# FOCUS ON
# RASHOMON

◆◆◆◆◆◆◆◆◆◆◆◆◆◆◆◆◆◆◆◆◆◆◆◆◆◆◆◆◆◆◆◆◆◆◆◆◆◆◆◆◆◆◆◆◆◆◆◆◆◆◆◆◆◆◆◆

*edited by*
*DONALD RICHIE*

A SPECTRUM BOOK

Prentice-Hall, Inc.
Englewood Cliffs, N.J.

*Library of Congress Cataloging in Publication Data*

RICHIE, DONALD.        comp.
  Focus on Rashomon.

  (Film focus) (A Spectrum book)
  Bibliography: p.
  1. Rashomon (Motion picture)    I. Title.
PN1997.R244R5        791.43′7        72–4555
ISBN 0–13–752980–5
ISBN 0–13–752972–4 (pbk.)

# FILM FOCUS

## Ronald Gottesman and Harry M. Geduld
### *General Editors*

DONALD RICHIE *is Curator of Film at The Museum of Modern Art,
New York City, and the recognized Western authority on Japanese
cinema. Author of many books on Japan and its films, he is perhaps
best known for* The Films of Akira Kurosawa.

Stills from *Rashomon* are reprinted by permission of Janus Films, Inc.,
and were supplied by Daiei Films, the Edward Harrison Estate, Janus
Films, Inc., and The Museum of Modern Art/Film Stills Archive New
York.

Printed in the United States of America

10    9    8    7    6    5    4    3    2    1

PRENTICE-HALL INTERNATIONAL, INC. (*London*)
PRENTICE-HALL OF AUSTRALIA, PTY. LTD. (*Sydney*)
PRENTICE-HALL OF CANADA, LTD. (*Toronto*)
PRENTICE-HALL OF INDIA PRIVATE LIMITED (*New Delhi*)
PRENTICE-HALL OF JAPAN INC. (*Tokyo*)

# CONTENTS

# ESSAYS

# ACKNOWLEDGMENTS

In preparing this volume I am indebted to Daiei Films, Janus Films, and, in particular, to the Film Study Center and Library of The Museum of Modern Art, New York. I am also grateful to Kinema Jumpo, Tadao Sato, and Akira Kurosawa.

# RASHOMON

## A Daiei Production

| | |
|---|---|
| DIRECTOR | Akira Kurosawa |
| PRODUCER | Jingo Minoru (later titles: Produced by Masaichi Nagata) |
| SCENARIO | Shinobu Hashimoto and Akira Kurosawa |
| PHOTOGRAPHY | Kazuo Miyagawa |
| ART DIRECTION | So Matsuyama |
| MUSIC | Fumio Hayasaka |

TIME: 88 MINUTES (2,406 METERS)

Released August 25, 1950. Distributed in the United States by Janus Films, Inc.

## CAST

| | |
|---|---|
| *Tajomaru, the bandit* | TOSHIRO MIFUNE |
| *Takehiro, the samurai* | MASAYUKI MORI |
| *Masago, his wife* | MACHIKO KYO |
| *The woodcutter* | TAKASHI SHIMURA |
| *The priest* | MINORU CHIAKI |
| *The commoner* | KICHIJIRO UEDA |
| *The police agent* | DAISUKE KATO |
| *The medium* | FUMIKO HOMMA |

# Introduction
## by DONALD RICHIE

*Rashomon* is a film that continues to be seen and studied in both the East and the West. Americans, Europeans, and Japanese continue to find in it an experience that is moving and provocative. That the East and the West find in this single film very different things indicates the complexity of the picture and the differences among the cultures. This introduction will attempt to elucidate these differences and, in so doing, perhaps provide a context for the *Rashomon* criticism that follows.

Kurosawa once, in another context, answered a question of mine about meaning by saying, "If I could have said it in words, I wouldn't have gone to the trouble and expense of making a film." *Rashomon,* no less than any of his pictures, is therefore an experience that the director would believe could not be verbalized— one created through those nuances, ambiguities, insights, of which film alone is capable. I asked him once about the meaning of *Rashomon.* He laughed and said, "Well, it's about this murder. . . ." The answer was only partially facetious. Kurosawa was indicating that the film was about its facts, and perhaps about the deductions one might draw from them. Once when I referred to the film in his hearing as *The Great Rashomon Murder Mystery,* he said, "That's really what we ought to have called it."

He was, to be sure, rather tired of and irritated with the many explanations of the picture, including my own—some of which you will read in succeeding pages. But beyond this, Kurosawa as a creator believes that the meaning of a film lies entirely within the experience of viewing that film. He dislikes and distrusts descriptions

1

of that experience and he particularly avoids any theoretical appreciation or criticism of film. *Rashomon* is a mystery story.

His opinion must be taken seriously. He is, after all, the creator of the film—he and his staff and cast. Further, just as he views the surface of his film and finds it complete (no mystery hidden under mystery), so the film itself—which so notoriously offers no help at all to the explicator—sees the surface of events and is quite content with that. There is, among the characters, some delving into motive and the like, but the film itself offers no apparent resolution. *The Great Rashomon Murder Mystery* remains unsolved.

One may deduce from this an assumption still common in the East, still commonly unknown in the West. There is in the East no traditional assumption of essence. One does not find ingrained belief in Truth or Beauty. Indeed, in the Japanese language such abstract nouns are rare. No one knows what Soul is in either hemisphere, but it is only in the East that no one cares. Personality itself is a concept that has only begun to exist in the countries of Asia; it is a rare Easterner who finds himself publicly unique in the American manner.

The Eastern assumption is that reality lies on the surface and that things are real, to this extent, all the way through. Our familiar concept of the face and mask is meaningless. The mask *is* the face. One may have, it is true, a choice of masks, and in that case, each becomes equally real. It is for this reason that ideas we would find antithetical are happily and simultaneously entertained. (For example, the average Japanese has a Shinto wedding and a Buddhist funeral, and perhaps a mild flirtation with Christianity along the way.)

Such an assumption—the assumption of *Rashomon,* that not only truth but any perception of reality is relative—the Westerner still finds uncomfortable. Western philosophy has led him to believe in inner realities, in Platonic ideals, and in rational thought. His religion has suggested that he believe in a complementary inner soul and hold rigid ideas of right and wrong.

Kurosawa would subscribe naturally to the Eastern assumption and would remain distrustful of any appreciation or criticism that sought for deeper meanings. The meaning, he has said, is there, on the surface.

Such an attitude is, of course, uncommon in the West, and both America and Europe have responded to *Rashomon* with a great deal of theoretical argument. Japan responded to the film in a somewhat different manner, as we will see. In general, however, the West recognized in this film something important about the East, and the East something important about the West. What this was is the burden of this introduction.

*Rashomon,* premiered in Tokyo on August 25, 1950, in New York on December 26, 1951 (after it had won the Venice Grand Prize for that year and just before it won the 1952 Academy Award for the Best Foreign Film), and first shown in Europe a bit later, had in the West a great critical impact. It was, particularly in the United States, puzzled over, wondered at, and turned this way and that in an effort to extract its "true" meaning. There is even now a continuing critical agreement that it is a puzzle picture, something to be solved.

There are various ways of discussing it, and the spectrum of opinion here published gives an indication of current and later reaction. Most of the reviews—from the late Richard Griffith's intelligent and generous appreciation, through the notorious review of John McCarten, so lacking in both these qualities—found the film attractively problematical. Later critical essays sought to discover, often in a surprisingly peevish manner, the "true" meaning. (Part of the ill temper displayed might have been caused by suspicions of inadequacy. Many are the apologies at knowing nothing about far Japan, and even more are the mistakes: The period of the film, variously reported as the eighth or ninth century, is actually the twelfth; Mifune was never "Kabuki trained"; Kurosawa is the director's family name; the Akutagawa originals were stories, not a novel; and so on.) An example of the search, one in which the humor is unintentional, is Pierre Mercier's recounting of the discussions, or lack of them, after the *Rashomon* showings at the apparently rather provincial Clermont-Ferrand Ciné-Club.

Various explanations have been reached. Some are historical, others are sociological, several verge on anthropology, some see allegory, although disguised. Almost everyone manages to find a message. Kurosawa himself suggested why when, in discussing his entire work with R. B. Gadi, he said that "whatever messages these films may have for the viewer have not been done intentionally. All kinds of people come to see a picture. And for all kinds of people, there are also all kinds of meanings. So it is with the pictures I make. If some see a message, it is because they are looking for one."

During the early 1950s, the West was certainly looking for a message. It was then that the most basic assumptions were beginning to be questioned. Mathematics, physics, anthropology, psychology—to name but several of the disciplines—had indicated that man and his world were far different from what had been commonly believed about them. Traditional religion and traditional philosophy were equally hard hit. Doubt and uncertainty were among the results, and for many, *Rashomon* seemed to both describe and comment upon the predicament of Western man.

It is for this reason that in criticism of the period and later, one finds stated or implied that *Rashomon* is about relative truth. At the time (and this is perhaps the reason for the popularity of the picture in Europe and America), in the teeth of ethical chaos, the film seemed to suggest—with its saved infant, its repentant woodcutter, its reaffirmed priest—a mild optimism. There is no Truth, the film seemed to say, only a number of truths; nevertheless, we should all take heart, because men can still love one another. The message had been discovered.

There is more to the film than this, however, since it is a genuine mystery. An assumption that Truth is being questioned and rendered relative leaves too much to be accounted for. One must next assume that here, as in all his later films, Kurosawa is commenting upon "reality," and not merely "truth." It is reality itself (that is, our apprehension of it) that is being questioned and rendered relative. At stake is the validity of subjective experience.

Although the West now accepts relative truth and even finds a certain comfort in the notion, the idea of relative reality remains

disturbing. Yet it is one that is quite taken for granted in Eastern
philosophy, religion, and aesthetics. If our apprehension of reality
is questioned, we, as unique and individual souls with separate personalities, feel insecure; if we relinquish our notions of soul and
individuality, however, we must admit that reality can, of itself, be
nothing if not multiple. My tree cannot be yours, since there is in
this universe no essence, only those codifications that we ourselves
make up, such as a category for trees. And it would follow, of course,
that my murder could not be yours. (Arguments better supporting
this assumption are found in Parker Tyler's essay on the film, and
in my own.)

The West has then found in *Rashomon* a description of its
dilemma and some arcane commentary upon it. It is also discovering, in the assumptions of the film, an interpretation of reality
radically different from any it itself has made, but one that suggests
an alternative mode of thought, one with which it is familiar in
Eastern aesthetics, in the Zen philosophy, in certain Indian sects,
and so forth.

The film remains a puzzle; and it is becoming more and more
apparent that this, indeed, is what it is intended to be—a mystery,
nothing more nor less.

In Japan the film also puzzled a few people. The producer himself said he had no idea what it was about, several critics could
make nothing of it, and a few enterprising theaters hired *benshi*
(those lecturer-commentators of the silent era) to inform and explain. Largely, however, although *Rashomon* was rightly judged
mysterious, the film was not regarded as a puzzle to be solved. It
was mysterious as life is mysterious.

What intrigued both the critics and the general audience was the
way in which the mystery was presented. They found the presentation analytic, logical, and speculative—qualities not nearly as common in Japan as elsewhere. The older critics consequently thought
the film far too "Western." One, finding that the picture questioned
reality and yet championed hope, said that that is not the Japanese
way, and he was quite correct. In this regard both Akutagawa and
Kurosawa are outside ordinary Japanese pragmatic morality, and

in this they do resemble the West more than they do the East. The Japanese audience, in other words, was quite ready to accept the story and its implications, but some of them could not understand the way the story was told—a situation precisely the opposite of that in the West.

Many other Japanese, however, were fascinated by the film. Some, like Akira Iwasaki, felt that here was an answer to one of the major problems of Japanese film aesthetics: how to be Japanese in a foreign art. (This is an important question in Japan, one difficult for us to understand until we realize how indelible the line is between things Japanese and things Western.) "In making films," says Iwasaki, "the Japanese are creating art in an imported medium with imported machinery and techniques. Where, then, do they come in as Japanese?" Iwasaki implies that this question is the most important of all to Kurosawa and that his films represent his answers to it. Concerning *Rashomon*, "the appeal of this style is that it views Japan through a kind of Western veil."

For the Japanese, then, the film represented an interesting and important experiment—the perfectly mundane notion that reality and/or truth is relative, demonstrated in an analytical, speculative, and otherwise attractively exotic manner—and one, moreover, that wedded the "foreignness" of cinema in general with the "Japaneseness" of Japanese art in particular. The West, as we have seen, found that the film represented an arresting and valuable work of art—a straightforward and logical recounting of certain events that led to the astonishing conclusion that there are no moral absolutes and that subjective apprehension was only one mode of comprehending reality, and not one of the more trustworthy ones at that.

This was not the first time that East and West found the diametrically opposite in the same object, but it must remain as one of the most typical. It also has, it must be said, very little to do with the film. *Rashomon* exists as an experience in itself. The invariably subjective interpretation is rendered more superfluous than usual, since the film is, among other things, a criticism of the subjective interpretation.

Among the problems experienced in collecting and presenting this material, there are several that remain unsolved. Almost all the reviewers find that they must give the story of the film before they can comment upon it. One could have cut out all these précis, but to do so would have been to deprive the authors of the grounds for some of their points, since—and I take this to be an indication of the validity of regarding *Rashomon* as being primarily about the relative nature of reality—some critics' versions of the story are different from those of others. Again, one of the problems is that, owing to the nature of *Rashomon,* most of the writers talk about what it says and not about how it says it, about what it is about and not about how it looks. For this reason, and in order to give the full story straight, among the essays on the film I first include my own.

Finally, I would direct the interested reader back to the film itself, distributed in the United States by Janus Films, and to its script, published by Grove Press, Inc., New York, as *Rashomon: A Film by Akira Kurosawa.*

# An Afternoon with Kurosawa

## by R. B. GADI

It is two-thirty, the afternoon of my appointment with the celebrated Japanese film director, Akira Kurosawa, who was in Manila
to receive the Ramon Magsaysay Memorial Award in Literature
and Journalism. It is the first time in eight years that this award—
named after the late Philippine President Magsaysay—is given to
someone in films. The last paragraph of the citation, like most documents of its kind, has tried to compress in a few words the significance of his work: "In electing Akira Kurosawa to receive the 1965
Award for Literature and Journalism, the Board recognizes his perceptive use of the film to probe the moral dilemma of man amidst
the tumultuous remaking of his values and environment of the mid-
20th century."

I am to meet him at three, ten minutes' ride from the office to his
hotel, but in this city, one can never be sure of the traffic. I sharpen
my pencils while waiting for the car, and on the way, I count the
light posts. Twenty-five posts and three o'clock, I knock on a door
at the end of a dark, L-shaped corridor. There are two men and
they rise as I come in. The younger one greets me and introduces
the director.

The room is thick with sun from two large windows that open to
the bay. On a table are two enormous bushes of yellow, pink, and
red gladioli with congratulation cards. The young man translates
my greeting. They get their coats from a closet beside the door and

*From* Solidarity *1, no. 1 (January/March 1966). Reprinted by permission.*

we walk out of the room for coffee and the interview. Kurosawa, the young man comments, likes the city, finds the room and the service just fine. No, he has not seen the country, may not have time to see it, and the heat occasionally bothers him. His height is arresting, his eyes soft, and his half-smile serious and yet familiar. At 56, his gait is that of 36, and his movements calm but energetic. The half-smile rests on his eyes while he talks, and a seriousness tinges his voice.

The coffee shop is quiet and is interrupted only by a uniformed man who screams at the phone. He watches amused, and I say that sometimes the heat brings hysterics.

"We all have hysterics," he answers, and slowly drinks his beer. He elaborates on hysterics. "There are so many things which portray violence," he says, "and so many films show this. Somehow, I feel tired of it." He wants his audience to leave the theatre entertained—with as little violence in the film as possible. "Although I do find it difficult to explain exactly what I mean by entertainment," he apologizes.

Is it close to being happy? He agrees. "It is easy to be happy. If it is necessary to show violence in a film, it is good to avoid ugliness." One notes this in several of his pictures: The cinematic devices create some amount of aesthetics in crises and tensions which are very close to outbursts. Here is art, without cloying subjectivity, but a disciplined absorption of all emotions through a unique communication, poignant and profound in both meaning and content. Spontaneity, in this sense, does not lose its essence.

This brings to mind the treatment of sex. If he avoids brutality, does he, too, avoid sex? The word amuses him, but his tone is unchanged. "There are already too many films that show sex. I do not want my films to be another vehicle for it." He pauses to light another cigarette. "Besides, I do not think it should be a purpose for entertainment. Children would not be able to understand it; it will only complicate their minds, and they will not be entertained."

And adults know too much about it, I go on. "Japan produces so many films on this," he says. "I think it is only *Rashomon* which has some sex in it."

Morality is an old obsession. But the exposition of Kurosawa's morality is unique. It is at once a blending of the ethic and the aesthetic. "Not even my religion interacts with my work. I remember what my mother used to tell me when I was a child. She said, 'Love of God and holiness should be kept within the heart.'"

For the artist must, by definition, be a strongly moral man, and his morality must be based on the code of his place and period, though frequently he may override it. "He may be pagan, oriental, or modern abstractionist," says Robert Coates, "yet he *must* pass judgment, if only—in case he belongs to the last category—by the kind and degree of order he may bring to his design." This is speaking of his work as an artist. Should Kurosawa's film speak of grace and holiness, it speaks from within his heart with a voice as soft as a child's.

Like *Ikiru,* I remind him, thinking of the old man Watanabe, 25 years "dead" with a cancerous stomach finally making him live to sing:

> Life is short,
> Fall in love, dear maiden,
> While your lips are still red,
> And before you are cold,
> For there will be no tomorrow,
> Life is so short,
> Fall in love, dear maiden,
> While your hair is still black,
> And before your heart withers,
> For today will not come again.

This life for the moment, as seen in *Ikiru*—is it an existentialist thought?

There is a hint of annoyance in his reply. "Existentialism? It is true that there is much I am not happy about with the way things are in this world—in Japan, particularly—but I do not want to show this unhappiness in my films." *Ikiru* is happy pathos, and "Japan particularly" in the film is a daily tragedy in a Public Works Office. But the moral greatness of the film cannot be overlooked. It is constantly reflected in the mirrors which tell too much on too many faces, in the children's laughter and the snow song at the swing. But there is no ascending the preacher's pulpit in Kurosawa; and this refusal to preach contributes to the beauty and the boldness of the picture. The dying Watanabe speaks to everyone in different manners, according to how and what one listens to. I hold on to Richard Brown's interpretation (quoted from Donald Richie's article on *Ikiru*):

> *Ikiru* is a cinematic expression of modern existentialist thought. It consists of a restrained affirmation within the context of a giant negation. What it says in starkly lucid terms is that "life" is meaningless when everything is said and done; at the same time one man's life can acquire meaning when he undertakes to perform some task which to him is meaningful. What everyone else thinks about that man's life is utterly beside the point, even ludicrous. The meaning of his act is what he commits the meaning of his life to be. There is nothing else.

*Ikiru,* or why the living is doomed, leaves no open wounds; even the death of Watanabe and the wake by the petty office-mates heal all scars. What remains, then, is what is taken *in toto,* not fragments, but a complete and painful realization of the whole of man, that his own slow decomposition becomes purely individual, and Kurosawa, by this time, is very far away from it.

Kurosawa sits behind the scenes, always patiently watching the actors on his stage. It is his words mouthed, his emotions prescribed on scripts, his makeup, his costumes, his voice that calls out whether a scene ought to be cut and retaken again; but the actor is left alone by himself to perform, not any director's life, but the life of man. And here lies the rub, because the viewer, too—for ill or good—despite the limitations or extensions of the cinema, participates. Subtlety is a Kurosawa art.

Folklore and certain beliefs of an esoteric society in the Japanese past have been brought out in a number of ways through the medium of the *Noh* and the *Kabuki* plays. Embodied in these theatrical arts—the dancing, the singing, and the instrumental music, all of which belong to a genre of their own—is the history of a people who were 12 centuries under China, 200 years in isolation, and finally, 15 years after they were crushed by a Western bomb, emerged as a nation whose living standards are far above the rest of Asia, and apparently competing with the West industrially. The cherry blossom season for modern Japan brings out the lessons of its history. Entertainment, like Japanese industry, seemed without sources in the past, and was largely directed to commercial and economic ends. Towards the latter part of the 19th century, the cinema was introduced in Japan. It was, at first, a wholly Western influence, until the diligence of the Japanese absorbed it to be one of their major forms of entertainment. The *Noh* plays continue to be shown but have decreased presentations according to seasonal activities; and the *Kabuki,* although the more popular form and still considered very much alive in Japan, has been designated to the *Kabuki-za* at the Ginza centers. Television and the motion picture are fast becoming the Japanese media for theatrical arts.

This is true not only with Japan. The West continues to be felt in Asia. But Japan struggles for her identity despite foreign influences, even in the field of entertainment. As expressed in the movies, the results of this self-reaffirmation appear like slapstick comedies; but it is consoling to note that, at least, there is a struggle. In the movies, particularly, there are several names which must be remembered to have brought the Japanese film some amount of prestige.

Akira Kurosawa did not consciously bear the responsibility of asserting his people's identity when he directed his first film. He merely intended to express himself. But because his works have been internationally acclaimed, one cannot help but place him with his people, or speak of him in relation to Asia. "It is a minor role I play," he insists humbly. And yet the minor role somehow gets the limelight. Which is true; a line can be drawn, as was done by his highly logical humanist critics, between his cinematographic art and himself as director. His films are a spectacle with a successful method of presentation, devoid of the grotesque.

This is not a revival of the *Noh,* although he affirms that the *Noh* is "very Japanese," but a revival of the drama, which has been a notable failure in films. His movies have developed their own way of telling a story, as in the theatre, but this is done with non-theatrical objects. The viability of the screen as a medium for drama is accomplished through the dialogue and the camera (included here are the projections). On this stage, the play is no longer of Japan, or of Asia, but of the world. It is only when one speaks of Kurosawa the director that we think of Japan's role in Asia and the world.

How far has Kurosawa reached? How much farther can he go? Of what value is a man with a message to a world engrossed in splitting more atoms or spending millions for monstrosities of a space race while "villagers" scamper about from starvation or from a fear of being plundered by barbarians? The villagers care only for their crops, and would readily kill their defenders because they are strangers and are strong. Still, the weak readily run to the strong in times of their own panic. And where are the samurai who will defend the villagers—is this a legend after all? There are no victors in a war, so the villagers sing; there is only the weeping for the dead. But do we still weep for the dead? Are there not enough stray dogs to amuse us and divert us away from weeping? This is the disease of the cities, the cancer of nations. But the doctors only hide behind the lies that the sickness is just a minor ulcer, we could go on living still and our children could go on being entertained by toy rabbits. The vomiting is nature's way—we have no reason to panic. And the Lady Macbeths—the petty evil elements that push a country to deeper evil—how perfectly expressionless are their masks—we do not know if they smile or weep. Whither, whither, shall we go; where is left, where is right, or is life just another cobweb forest shrouded with thick mist and a fog that chokes us so that we lose our way? Is not home, too, a confused castle with horses and soldiers running about hysterically? Will there be a time when we can wash our hands clean of blood and not go insane? . . .

Kurosawa is a director amazingly articulate, with a voice for all people. Perhaps the strain in his eyes is not a strain of age, but a weariness with the world. But sadly for most of us, this ennui has become no longer a feeling, but a fad.

He lights a cigarette and stares through the glass window at the cars that continuously pass. He breathes deeply. Again, he smiles. "There is no rest for this kind of life. But I am happy with it. I work for months on a script before I feel that it is ready for a film. And this is the case with all my films. I think of them again and again even in my dreams. Sometimes while shooting a film, I am still bothered by a film I had finished months earlier."

The sun sets slowly and the grass outside that looked a brighter green is now paler. "I run away from the sets and the noise of the studio by playing golf." A fine way to run, I say; you hit the ball follow it, hit it again and curse if you either hit it too hard or not hard enough.

"But again, I do not think my thoughts would ever leave me. Even when playing golf, I also think of what to do next with a film or a scene-taking. I am beginning to believe that I have become a better golfer than director."

It has been a life of film making, indeed. He began this involvement while in his early twenties, working at first in different departments of a movie company, and eventually directing and producing films himself. "I have never thought of doing anything else aside from this. Not even play directing." This is unusual, considering his deep admiration for the *Noh* play, and the noticeable influence the *Noh* has in his adaptation of Macbeth (*The Throne of Blood*).

"I am very careful with influences," he comments. "I do not want a film to be obviously an influence of something or the other. As a matter of fact I do not even want to be obsessed with a message, for such an obsession may delimit the film into doing nothing but carry a message. Again, every film cannot help having influences. I have learned very much while working with Kajiro Yamamoto, but influence is a different thing altogether. I work in a manner distinct from him."

He draws an imaginary line across the table from his frothed glass to the ash tray. Is there a distinction between the artist and external influences? The *Noh* play, religion, foreign films and foreign stories, contemporary Japan and the rich Japanese history all work their way into his films, but it is always with detachment that the integration is treated. The characters move by themselves, the film grows by itself. Even Macbeth in *The Throne of Blood* is not circumscribed by Shakespeare's England. Like Hamlet, who also appeals to him, Macbeth belongs to no particular period. The *kyogen* dance in the banquet scene says:

> All of you wicked, listen while
> I tell of a man, vain
> sinful, vile—
> who, though ambitious, insolent,
> could not escape his punishment.

Caught between the spirits of evil and the little good that remains inside him, it is mist and rain and fog for Macbeth, and he is lost both in the forest and in his own castle, and his actions seem meaningless and limited. He is constantly running but to nowhere—like the horse outside his room that runs in circles; he is constantly moving, but all places limit him—his room, the castle, the forest are not far enough to run to, and none of these give respite to his troubled soul.

The camera, like Kurosawa, is farthest from the character's faces when they start writhing and their faces distort in confusion or indecision. And yet all this is without pain: the murder of the king, Lady Macbeth's delivery of a stillborn, etc. And if there is pain in Macbeth as a hundred arrows pierce him, his eyes stare, his mouth stiffens, and he merely pants like a dog. Not once does he cry for help. Suffering is most tragic if it is no longer human, and Macbeth's dying is like that of a hunted beast. Lady Asaji (Lady Macbeth) is a perfect *Noh* character. She minces about her limited stage, sly and as evil as a fourth Shakespearean witch. Whither, whither? is all that the film could ask. The soul is trapped by evil —whither, whither—and even with Macbeth's death, the furies would have sung:

> Still his spirit walks, his fame is known,
> for what once was, is now yet true—
> murderous ambition will pursue . . .

Your films do carry messages, I insist. He swallows hard and looks again at the grass outside, which is now almost black because the sun has completely set.

"Whatever messages these films may have for the viewer have not been done intentionally. All kinds of people come to see a picture. And for all kinds of people, there are also all kinds of meanings. So it is with the pictures I make. If some see a message, it is because they are looking for one." Although cinema is not always reputed as art, this is the value of art: It is capable of being conceived in a variety of manners, depending on the viewer, and its value lies between its creativity and its control.

"Art in film?" He looks around the room and lets his eyes rest on the sugar bowl. "Again, I would not know how to answer that. Art is something perfect, beautiful, and rather difficult to achieve. I believe that art cannot be achieved completely, although I try very hard. I do not agree with critics who say that I have achieved a perfect union between art and film making. Everytime I finish a film, I say to myself that my next film should do better. So you see, it is a constant effort to do something better. I don't think I will ever stop and say I finally did it."

There are elements which tend to disturb the value of a film, regardless of how well written the scripts are or how well directed the movie is. The value of a film—whether it be intended to entertain or not—depends on the choice and reason for its subject matter. The cinema does not necessarily have to appeal merely to sight and hearing, but to thought and feeling as well. Here lies the most delicate angle for a film—to be considered not only a good work, but a work of value.

In the case of Kurosawa, the work on a film is not only the role of film director, but also that of script writer, makeup artist, camera man, choreographer, artist, or singer. He revises scripts (be they patterned after a play, as in *The Throne of Blood,* which is Shakespeare's; or a story, as in *Stray Dog,* which is Simenon-influenced; or a legend, as in *Seven Samurai*), consults makeup artists, sits with the camera, chooses the dances and the songs and the scenery to be shot. "But what is really most important is the thought that I want to say." What matters then is not where the story or the script came from, but what it wants to tell.

*Ikuru* is his own meditation upon death. It is a personal labor between what he is doing and what he really *wants* to do. "I feel that there is still so much I have to do, and yet have done so little. I think I have not lived enough, but I try not to be sad." So *Ikuru* was written and produced according to this thought. It is the problem of living and of identification.

*Stray Dog,* although a Simenon infatuation, "is quite true." It was his idea to present a "real detective who lost his pistol." Despite incongruities and inconsequentials, it still came out as an excellent idea: "Why is it that the truly good are not identical?" To quote Richie again, "by suggesting that good and evil, cops and robbers, are one, he has shown us that we are in ourselves both good and evil, both cop and robber. The difference among these is not one of essence. It has to do merely with identity. The character of the murderer is indeed the most important because it is only he (among others in the film) who made the choice not to hunt, not to find himself, not to persevere, not to believe."

*Seven Samurai* is a historical film based after the *jidai-geki,* on the period films; but what Kurosawa wanted to bring out was the meaning of these samurai and their relevance to the present. It is not, therefore, a historical documentary, but something alive that will speak of a tragedy which Kurosawa has made into a cinematic masterpiece.

Although Kurosawa was intrigued by Hamlet, he felt that Macbeth's story had more appeal, because it did not involve the audience too much in deep thought. But why Macbeth particularly, of all of Shakespeare's characters? To quote Donald Richie again, "Kurosawa saw in Macbeth a contemporary issue—a parallel between medieval Japan and medieval Scotland which illuminated contemporary society; and further, a pattern which is valid in both historical and contemporary contexts."

"I look at life," comments Kurosawa, "as an ordinary man. I simply put my feelings into the film. When I look at Japanese history—or the history of the world for that matter—what I see is how man repeats himself over and over again."

Why the choice and why the reason, one sees these in his films. He tries to explain these, operating only with tradition and a refined imagination. Economy and precision are still his most artistic.

He uses the commonest, the simplest, the nearest at hand; he refrains from broad farces; he becomes highly cultured without being oversophisticated. If there are faults inherent in the films, the virtues on the other hand are very exceptional. And to appreciate his movies calls for new attitudes toward the film as art.

"I cannot, as yet, speak of any forthcoming film. At the moment I am still recovering from the surprise at getting this award."

The award overwhelms him. "I can use the money for another film," he adds. He is more happy than afraid of having to stand before an audience to deliver a speech on the evening of the award ceremony. "This is the first time that I am directed what to do on stage. I am awkward in front of a crowd." But home is where the work is, and a few days in a different city is not really respite from the job. The wife is a silent critic, and the two children, he is glad, do not share the burden of his thoughts. A nineteen-year-old son sings his folk songs ("I, too, enjoy folk songs aside from the classics, and I do hope to see Joan Baez when she comes to Japan."), and an eleven-year-old daughter is busy with school. Nine o'clock at the studio, shots taken, scripts revised, locations located, places and people and actors—this is home; this is Japan.

Japan is also an emotion. The Japanese are again developing a consciousness for history, and modern Japan in its variety recedes occasionally into the past. In 1894, after more than two centuries of the Tokugawa Shogunate's seclusion, Japan began absorbing Western technology. A few years after this awakening, the Japanese film industry started. Today there are several names to remember in the Japanese film world—Ozu, Mizoguchi, Inagaki, Kinugasa, Yoshimura, and Kurosawa, who brought international prestige to the Japanese film industry in 1952 by winning the Venice International Film Festival's Grand Prize with Daiei's *Rashomon*.

Despite competition with the television and a film-hungry public which compels production companies to "turn out films simply to feed the cinema chains," the Japanese film industry has a future delicately guided by its present film directors. It is a future that could turn anywhere, according to the temper of its directors and the demands of technique and trade. Kurosawa may yet stand out as Japan's most dynamic director and one of the greatest in the world cinema.

"I can only do my best," he says humbly. "The making of a film industry demands very much, and it is not often a happy approval that one gets from oneself."

I recall *Stray Dog* and the unhappiness that he voiced about the film. "It is just too technical. All that technique and not one real thought in it." Obviously, this time, his thoughts were not clearly said in the film. The picture is concerned with the search for a pistol clumsily lost by a detective; the story unfolds as the pursuit of subject and object, the confusion between animate and inanimate. Like the Simenon novel, which Kurosawa said he "did not quite achieve," the inconsequentials reveal an uncanny importance. Eventually, the distinction between pursued and pursuer is blurred. Here is a compromise between man and his virtue, and even if Kurosawa himself is not too happy about this film, it doubtlessly leaves a clear picture of postwar Tokyo, almost "Balzacian in its variety," a city stretching out from the slums, striptease joints, and geisha houses. This could be a picture of Manila, too; malevolent, corrupt, and straining for some semblance of affluence and order.

"But my failure to put my thoughts on film is not my only problem in a production. There are the time element, the problem of materials, setting, and actors. As far as actors are concerned, I look for those who have as little self-consciousness as possible." And when he does find them, they are made to suit the roles afforded them, and like Mifune, the relationship between director and actor lasts for a great number of years.

Kurosawa toys casually with a cigarette before lighting it. "It takes so much to put out a film, aside from the energy one dedicates to it. I have made around two dozen films—I can't remember exactly how many—and some film scripts alone take more than a year to finish. There is *Seven Samurai*, a film which has come out as Tokyo's most expensive film to date. Aside from the financial difficulties, there were the scenes which were difficult to shoot, the weather which was always bad, the lack of materials and props, like horses." Despite these, he went on filming.

"I have always wanted to put out a real period film." Other producers have done so, but again, Kurosawa did not want to stop at a period; instead he wanted to make the past relevant and significant, so that it shows not as a historical documentary, but as an important transition from that period to the present, shorn of the time element, and imbued with universality.

"The American copy (*The Magnificent Seven*) is a disappointment, although entertaining. It is not a version of *Seven Samurai*. I do not know why they call it that. Oh, but I do enjoy some American films," he adds hurriedly. "But I do not remember their titles. I am partial to European films." He mentions several names: Fellini, de Sica, Kazan, and a film, *The Red Balloon*.

It is dark outside, and the lights are dim in the coffee shop. We can no longer distinguish the grass from the night. More people come in, and we have had a potful and almost a caseful of coffee and beer. "Although whiskey is my favorite," he adds.

"My thoughts are better expressed in my films. And I am sure that what I say in my films I cannot say in any other way."

We all stand and he offers a handshake. It is a cold hand I take, but there is warmth in his smile. I leave Kurosawa and hail a cab. It does not matter if the traffic takes me more than half an hour to get back to the office. On the way, I do not count the light posts any more.

# Kurosawa and His Work
## by AKIRA IWASAKI

**1**

Akira Kurosawa has already been at work on his latest film, *Akahige* (*Redbeard*), for more than a year. Even allowing for a break occasioned by brief illness, this is unusually long for the making of a Japanese film, and the reason lies, above all, in the perfectionism which characterizes all Kurosawa's creative activity. For instance, on a site close to the Toho studios, he has had his architect build for him an exact replica of a charity hospital of the late Tokugawa Period, an old-style, one-storied building with a tiled roof. Not only is this structure faithful to the contemporary plans, but anybody willing to forego various modern comforts could actually live in it for months on end.

The film takes place in the period when Western medicine was first transplanted to Japan and began to take root. Those young medical students of the day who were dissatisfied with the traditional Oriental medicine imported from China many centuries previously would make their way to the port of Nagasaki, the only point of contact with Western culture in a Japan officially isolated from the rest of the world. There they would study for several years and, on their return to Edo, apply their knowledge of the most up-to-date medical treatment for the benefit of the common people. The hero of the film, the head of a charity hospital, known by the nickname of Redbeard, is such a man. He himself has been to study

*From* Japan Quarterly *12, no. 1 (January/March 1965). Reprinted by permission of the author. Translated by John Bester.*

at Nagasaki in his youth, and it is at his hospital that the young Noboru, his at first rebellious but later faithful follower, unpacks his bags on his return from a similar mission. Undoubtedly, Kurosawa's interest was stirred by the prospect of portraying these two humanist scientists who stood at the dawn of Japan's modern age. Yet was there not, perhaps, another, more personal motive behind his choice of such a theme?

While it is Akira Kurosawa who today represents the Japanese art of the film in the eyes of the world, it does not follow that in Japan itself he is considered a truly Japanese artist. Not a few Japanese, in fact, would ascribe his world fame precisely to his "non-Japanese" qualities.

In an exchange of letters between Kurosawa and myself, published by a Japanese magazine some time ago, Kurosawa declares:

"I am a man who enjoys Basho and Buson along with Dostoevski, who likes Sotatsu, Gyokudo, and Tessai in the same way as Van Gogh, Lautrec, and Rouault. . . . I collect old Japanese lacquerware as well as antique French and Dutch glassware. In short, the Western and the Japanese live side by side in my mind naturally, without the least sense of conflict."

To a certain extent, any average intellectual in Japan today could confess to being in the same position; the ordinary dilettante, indeed, can perfectly well combine Japan and the West without feeling bothered at all. However, for a creative artist of Kurosawa's caliber it is not such a simple matter. The two things, the Western and the Japanese, certainly do exist alongside in him, but their coexistence is marked by constant conflict and sparring and, when they do make contact and combine with each other, by showers of sparks and the generation of much heat and light. Compared with directors of an earlier generation such as the late Yasujiro Ozu and Mikio Naruse, who are reputed to be the most "Japanese" of all film-makers, and with whom Japan is part of the very fiber of their being, Kurosawa belongs to a more recent generation which must look to the West for help in defining Japan, which verifies and analyzes the one by constant reference to the other.

The very first scenario Kurosawa ever wrote (written while he was still an assistant director, it never reached the screen) was "The German of Dharma Temple," which portrayed the life in Japan of Bruno Taut, the celebrated German architect. The choice of subject bears witness to a constant preoccupation of Kurosawa's, from his youth right up to the present. It was Taut, one of the founders of the Bauhaus, who discovered the plain and simple beauty of the Japanese sense of form to which the Japanese themselves, overfamiliar, had become apathetic, and brought it once more into the Japanese consciousness. The process constituted a second rediscovery of Japan by the Japanese; the first was the reawakening prompted by the American art critic Fenollosa at the end of the nineteenth century. Kurosawa, too, as a young art student was much occupied with the question of the precise meaning of "Japanese," and he felt an interest in Taut as pointing the way to an answer. He discovered in Taut an instructive counterpart.

It was via such devious routes as this that the modern Japanese who had experienced fascination and infatuation for Western civilization had to hunt after, or find his way back to, the truly "Japanese." In this sense, "The German of Dharma Temple," though no more than a study, represents something essential in Kurosawa; it was an attempt by the youthful Korosawa, using Taut as a medium, to come to terms with his own past. *Sanshiro Sugata* (1943) —his first film, which brought him his first success—tells how the hero, Sanshiro, is ordered by his teacher to spend a whole day and night up to his neck in a lotus pond, as a result of which he grasps the essential secret of judo. The film seeks to embody this surely Japanese idea of a truth to be attained through sudden enlightenment or through rigid self-discipline—an idea, incidentally, which is obviously related to the Zen concepts fashionable at the moment.

In *Redbeard,* Kurosawa's interest is directed toward the confrontation between Japan and the West in the feudal society of a century or so ago, and toward the ways in which the West prodded Japan into motion and Japan, on her side, gradually set about assimilating the West. The fact that the hero is known by the name Redbeard, which was applied to all Westerners at the time, is in itself symbolic. It is true that Redbeard is convinced of the superiority of Western medicine, and is forever studying so as not to be left behind by its constant advances, yet in other respects he is a Japanese through and through. This is demonstrated most clearly of all by the purely Japanese way in which he teaches Noboru, the pupil for whom he feels most affection and on whom he pins most hopes: He gives him not a single word of instruction or advice, but relies solely on silent practice and precept to convey his influence.

*Kumonosu-jo* (*The Throne of Blood*, 1957) is, of course, Kurosawa's version of *Macbeth*. In it, he consciously adopts stylistic elements from the *Noh*, yet this is no mere trick, no feeling of "Well, this is a Shakespeare classic, so let's have a bit of classic *Noh* style to match." Even if it was so at the beginning, in the course of long and careful rehearsals with all his actors—something no other director in Japan does—Kurosawa was led by his fastidious sense of style to the idea of giving the work unity as a Japanese film by the use of motifs from the *Noh*.

In making films, the Japanese are creating art in an imported medium with imported machinery and techniques. Where, then, do they come in as Japanese? Where is the evidence that they are Japanese? This is a question that constantly preoccupies Kurosawa. What makes it more difficult is the fact that the Japanese outlook he must express will not be genuine unless it loves not only Basho and Sotatsu but Van Gogh and Rouault as well. That theme, which first appears in "The German of Dharma Temple," persists through *The Throne of Blood* and right up to *Redbeard*.

It is not possible to discuss *Redbeard* stylistically, since nobody has seen it yet. *The Throne of Blood,* however, was an unprecedented work in that, although its subject matter was regrettably no more than a rehash of *Macbeth,* stylistically it was an experiment with national and classical styles in the Japanese cinema.

The appeal of this style is that it views Japan through a kind of Western veil. It was for much the same reason that *Rashomon,* which first established Kurosawa as a director of international stature when it took the Grand Prix at the Venice Film Festival, won such praise among Western critics despite the fact that in Japan it was not considered such a great masterpiece—the Japanese critics voted it to fourth or fifth place among the films of that year.

## 2

The popular appeal of Kurosawa's films lies first and foremost in their ability to tell a good story. With only one or two exceptions, his films have all been commercial successes. Again in strong contrast with such "Japanese" artists as Ozu and Naruse, he is drawn toward everything that is unusual, nonroutine, or abnormal, and he relates these things via techniques that seek constantly to startle.

One day many years ago, a young clerk in a trading company, unknown both to him and the world at large, brought him a scenario to read. As he read, Kurosawa was fascinated by the way each scene presented a challenge to the audience and each sequence had its quota of surprise and suspense. Here, at last, was the ideal type of scenario for him. In this way, Shinobu Hashimoto became Kurosawa's most trusted staff writer, and the scenario in question appeared shortly as the film *Rashomon*.

Nevertheless, unlike a crafty veteran of commercial storytelling such as Alfred Hitchcock, Kurosawa does not attach the ultimate importance to storytelling and clever strokes in the unfolding of the tale. Rather he is concerned with the inner significance of the story.

*Rashomon* is too well known to need much discussion here. In it, Kurosawa sets forth four accounts of a murder which takes place in a bamboo grove, given respectively by a bandit, the samurai who is killed, the samurai's wife who is violated by the bandit, and a woodcutter who witnesses the incident. Through these differing accounts, he seeks to demonstrate the many-sided nature of truth and, at a deeper level, its essential relativity—the nonexistence anywhere of any absolute truth. It was the nihilism and mistrust of humanity apparent in the tale that were to drive the original author, Ryunosuke Akutagawa, to despair and suicide. Unfortunately, they are utterly at variance with the outlook of Kurosawa himself, who is a humanist at heart. So, in the final scene of the film, he cannot resist having second thoughts and making the woodcutter, prompted by the stirrings of conscience, take up an abandoned child with the intention of bringing it up. Thus he gives the final victory to good will and neighborly love, although this ending clearly does violence to the whole philosophy of the film.

The thing which distinguishes Akira Kurosawa from other Japanese directors—I would go so far as to call it his great achievement —is precisely that he is first and foremost a director of ideas. Kurosawa is fond of insisting that every artist has, ultimately, only one theme. In his own case, he says, it is the question of why men cannot live together more happily and with greater good will than they do. Of course, one should be wary of swallowing whole such self-revelations by artists, since the artist is prone to self-delusion and self-misinterpretation in peculiarly complex and involved forms. Nevertheless, Kurosawa's remark can be taken at its face value insofar as it suggests that all his works are born, originally, of an idea. Whereas Japanese film directors in the past have leaned heavily toward naturalism, basing their work on a narrow, personalized experience, Kurosawa's style is intellectual, and his emergence after the war marked the appearance of an utterly unfamiliar element in the Japanese film world.

The fact that his favorite author is Dostoevski is in itself enough to suggest his style. Most of his films have a theme expressible in one line, or even one word: good, evil, happiness, unhappiness, the beauty of love—problems that boil down in essence to the problems of the existence of man, its meaning and its forms. Some of his titles, such as *Ikiru* (*To Live,* 1952) and *Ikimono no Kiroku* (*Record of a Living Being,* 1955), frankly set forth this concern from the very start. In *Donzoko* (*The Lower Depths,* 1957) he sets out again to study the conditions for man's survival in, as it were, a sealed room, and it troubles him very little that his story leans heavily in its outlines on a work by a Western writer, Gorky.

Kurosawa is a research worker who places man in a test tube, provides certain conditions or applies certain stimuli, then waits to see his reaction. His films are the resulting case studies. For example, he unearths an honest workman who finds himself one Sunday morning with only 35 yen in his pocket, in a great city plagued with the inflation and black marketeering of the immediate postwar years. What joys and what sorrows will the day bring him and his sweetheart? This is the experiment that produced *Subarashiki Nichiyobi* (*One Wonderful Sunday*, 1947).

*To Live* is still more frankly a case history: What effect does the news that he has only six months to live have on a man? Will he give himself over in despair to debauchery and dissolute living, or will he try to pass his remaining days as gracefully and meaningfully as he can? Kanji Watanabe, a middle-aged government clerk, is singled out as the hero. Twenty-five years of his life he had spent sitting at a desk in a city hall, mechanically applying his seal to the documents placed before him: the classic type of the "hollow man" who cannot, not for one moment of that time, ever be said to have "lived." One day at the hospital, he is told that he has stomach cancer and is given only three or four months to live. For the first time he becomes conscious of life, and begins to dwell on its significance. In the face of death, the man who for decades has not lived begins to live for the first time. He stops applying his seal mechanically to his official documents, conceives an affection for a girl young enough to be his granddaughter, and devotes every hour of his short remaining life to constructing for her a park no larger than a pocket handkerchief in a corner of the city. The evening of the day on which the park is completed finds him seated on a swing flecked with snow, ready now to meet his end with tranquillity. The small flame that has flared momentarily at the end of a small man's life is yet, for all its smallness, a sign that Kanji Watanabe has lived.

If *To Live* is Kurosawa's finest work, *Tengoku to Jigoku* (*High and Low*, 1963) is comparatively confused. He uses the second-rate American mystery on which it is based merely as a springboard for his ideas on and criticisms of the modern age. In form a crime film, it is in that sense a struggle of wits and of wills between detective and criminal, a guessing game played between director and audience. In fact, however, Kurosawa uses this interest as a way of presenting his objections to and mistrust of the contemporary social structure. Here are the pitiless rules of modern capitalism. Here are the extreme material abundance and the absolute poverty that is its reverse face—though Kurosawa, carefully avoiding class references, refers to the contrasting sides of life simply as "heaven" and "hell." Here, too, is a modern Raskolnikov, who, living in the midst of it all yet priding himself on his superhuman wisdom and morality, takes his revenge on the social structure, and, in order to demonstrate the absolute infallibility of his own brain, resorts to murder and extortion. Set against this figure of evil is an honest manufacturer who is forced to give up all his property for the sake of his chauffeur's son, kidnaped by mistake for his own. The question that Kurosawa poses here is how far man is responsible for his neighbor and for the life and safety of others who are human like himself. He goes further and raises the question, Is not a man who is rich *ipso facto* guilty of a kind of original sin?

In *High and Low,* unfortunately, the question does not get across very strongly. Some, possibly correctly, have seen in the film a compromise with commercialism. In the earlier *Warui Yatsu Hodo Yoku Nemuru (The Bad Sleep Well,* 1960), however, Kurosawa had dug boldly to the roots of the major evils afflicting modern Japan —graft, bureaucratism, corruption within the political parties, and big-time Capital pulling the strings of government. In *Redbeard,* Kurosawa makes it clear that the enemy confronting both Redbeard himself and Noboru is not simply disease but a political setup which creates poverty and ignorance without the means to remedy them.

### 3

Even the characters who appear in Kurosawa's films seem to be internalized, to have passed through the filter of his intellect, and in the actors Toshiro Mifune and Takashi Shimura he has found the ideal vehicles for his ideas. Again and again they appear: the consumptive gangster Matsunaga with an inner loneliness belying outward swagger, and the boozy doctor Sanada who tends him so carefully, cursing him vilely all the while (*Drunken Angel,* 1948); the corrupt lawyer Hiruta who will stoop to any infamy in order to get money for the treatment of the consumptive daughter whom he worships (*Scandal,* 1950); Nakajima, the old man who in his opposition to nuclear tests—"Dying is one thing, but I'm damned if I'll be killed"—proposes to abandon family and wealth and go to live on the other side of the globe, and who ends up in a room in a lunatic asylum, pointing to the sunset and crying, "The world is on fire!" (*Record of a Living Being*); or Sanjuro, who turns up out of nowhere, weeds out the petty gangsters who lord it over the local community, then drifts off to the next small town in the same way he came (*Yojimbo*, 1961; *Tsubaki Sanjuro*, 1962).

Kurosawa always speaks of *Hakuchi* (*The Idiot*, 1951) with the greatest affection, though it is generally accounted one of his failures. Here, as in his version of *Macbeth*, it was an intellectual outlook on mankind already laid down in the original work that attracted his interest and stimulated his creativity. With *The Lower Depths* (1957), the thing that inspired him was the way Gorky takes the ordinary Russian people toward the end of the Czarist era and, placing them in an isolated setting, uses them as a kind of pure culture for his experiment. During a conversation I had with him in Warsaw last year, Andrzei Wajda, the great Polish director, who had high praise for Kurosawa, remarked that Nishi, the hero of Kurosawa's *The Bad Sleep Well* (1960) was a reincarnation in modern Japan of Hamlet. It had never occurred to me personally, but the remark undoubtedly revealed a grasp of the spring of Kurosawa's creativity.

Nor is it only Kurosawa's characters that are intellectually conceived. The settings in themselves seem somehow removed from the ordinary, everyday dimension. The very air is denser, the air pressure greater than in the atmosphere we normally breathe, sounds fall on the ear an octave higher than their usual pitch, and physical movements are speeded up or slowed down abnormally. Without such an atmosphere and such a setting, in fact, his characters would be incapable of acting freely or naturally. His films, simply described, are dramas of violent emotions, their traumatic effect heightened still further by exaggeration, emphasis, and extremes. Kurosawa himself admits to a preference for the harsher aspects of nature—for the glitter of high summer and the asperity of midwinter, for torrential rains and blizzards. They provide his films with their natural backdrop and, of course, with their psychological background as well. They are the reverse of the conventionally "Japanese"—of the equivocal, the understated and the unadorned. He rejects the traditional "boiled-rice-and-green-tea" austerity so beloved of Ozu and Naruse: "I want my films to be like a steak spread with butter and topped with good, rich, broiled eels."

I have described his style as intellectual, a label which he gives to his work himself. Yet, in another aspect, the excellence of his work derives from the acuteness with which he constantly observes, remembers, and records the external world. He keeps an avid eye on the society and men about him, ever ready to summon actuality to amend his ideas for him.

During the filming of *Rashomon,* while Kurosawa's staff was at a loose end in its Kyoto hotel waiting for the completion of an open-air set, the half-ruined gateway that was to become famous all over the world, they saw a 16-mm. film of an expedition to Africa. One shot showed a lion staring at the cameraman from the edge of the jungle. "Look, Mifune!" cried Kurosawa. "That's how Tajomaru should be!" In that instant, he had seen the bandit Tajomaru as he was to appear in the film, peering out at the woman with piercing eyes from the bamboo grove. Around the same time, Masayuki Mori, who played the part of the murdered samurai Kanazawa no Takehiro, saw a film featuring a black panther at one of the local cinemas, and at his recommendation they all went to see it. When the panther at last appeared, Machiko Kyo, the actress who played the part of the young wife Masago, covered her face with her hands in alarm. It was this gesture that crystallized in Kurosawa's mind the image of Masago, confronted by the two men fighting over her like wild beasts in a thicket.

Kurosawa always insists that no amount of intellectualization can substitute for the living human being. When he succeeds, it is because the careful eye he keeps trained on reality is preventing ideas from running away with him.

When Kurosawa begins writing a scenario, he has no idea of what the final scene will be; intellectual though his first inspiration may be, he abhors intellectual conclusions. He creates the setting and gives his characters their personalities, but from then on it is the characters themselves who, with unpredictable results, take over the action. A single passing remark is enough to set his heroes and heroines on a completely different course, and he is obliged to follow them wherever they lead. It is this kind of realism in the course of creation that gives a sense of actuality to the nonrealistic worlds he creates.

Unfortunately, a work produced in this fashion sometimes ends up at a point that conflicts with the film's original intellectual point of departure. At such times, the original idea is left stranded and without support. At the end of *Rashomon,* the itinerant priest who has listened to the whole story states that, thanks to the woodcutter, he has regained his temporarily shaken faith in humanity— a conclusion utterly out of keeping with the main theme the film has gone to such trouble to expound, the relativity of truth and the perfidy of man. At the end of *Seven Samurai* (1954), Kambei, the most clever strategist of the band, who has rid the farming village of the wandering samurai who have been preying on it, muses to himself as he rides away: The samurai have passed away like the wind, while the peasants, like the earth itself, go on forever—a patently forced moral that blends ill with what has gone so far. It is, as it were, a vestigial reminder of the original idea that moved Kurosawa to make the film.

# REVIEWS

# RICHARD GRIFFITH

◆◇◆◇◆◇◆◇◆◇◆◇◆◇◆◇◆◇◆◇◆◇◆◇◆◇◆◇◆◇◆◇◆◇◆◇◆◇◆◇◆◇◆◇◆

The release of any good Japanese film in the United States is news; the arrival of a great one is sensational. *Rashomon* is, for my money, a great film, and the mystery is, where did it come from? It breaks entirely with Japanese film-making tradition, and its editing structure, camera work, and acting challenge comparison with the outstanding film achievements in any country or period. Its greatest novelty is its story, which is non-national, timeless, and universal. More, it is a story about men and women—about sex—and it results, unless I am very much mistaken, in one of the two or three films ever made for grownups, instead of for kiddies six to sixty.

It concerns a double crime—a rape and a murder—told from four points of view, those of the three participants and of an onlooker. The three involved soften their versions to come off as well as possible in their own eyes as well as those of the court before whom they speak. The onlooker's version is presumably the correct one, although he, too, turns out to have been secretly involved in the horrifying scene which he witnessed and which haunts his conscience. These four complex variations on the same theme are unique for the fluidity of their narration, for the clarity of their interrelationship, and for the suspense they build; the film is an editorial tour de force and dramatically draws attention to this crucial function of the movie director. Certainly no director now at work has a better grasp of structure than the unknown (in the West) Akira Kurosawa, whose many talents merit a more complete descrip-

*From* Saturday Review, *January 19, 1952. Copyright 1952 The Saturday Review Associates, Inc. Reprinted by permission.*

tion than space permits. Since it is impossible to deal with them all, I focus here on the aspect which I think will interest American audiences most, the acting—or, better, Kurosawa's handling of his players.

The acting in *Rashomon* doesn't resemble that in other Japanese films I have seen, which is chiefly derived from the traditional theatre of Japan. Neither is it like stage or screen acting in the contemporary West. It is more like silent film acting than anything else I can think of, and how people will judge it is anybody's guess. In the 1921 *Tol'able David,* there is a scene in which Ernest Torrence, the villain, prepares to fight the hero. As he nerves himself to the attack, a muscle in his face twitches uncontrollably. When this film is shown nowadays at the Museum of Modern Art, most audiences react to the face-twitching with laughter. They have forgotten—the conventions of present-day acting have made them forget—that under the stress of fear or anger, a man loses control of his nervous system. His pulse pounds, his heart beats faster, adrenalin pumps through him, he is apt to shake and make unintelligible noises. He cannot disguise what he feels. Speech is a method for disguising emotion as well as expressing it, and since dialogue dominates most films today, the ability of silent screen actors to exhibit naked emotion has become a forgotten art which is not even recognized as an art when occasionally resurrected.

*Rashomon* is a reminder of what it was like at its best, and this is no accident. It is part of the design of the film. The three participants in the murder describe it eloquently in words, but their eloquence is false. Like convicts "playing with the evidence," they dress up their stories to their advantage. But when we see what really happened, verbal narration is abandoned, and the camera speaks as only it can. In this harrowing scene, both elemental and sophisticated, the disguises are stripped away and two men and a woman are revealed to one another in a light none of them can bear. All that has gone before was an attempt to mask that revelation, which is simply that "the human heart is hollow and full of filth." But also this strange, profound film reminds us at the very end the heart can be uplifted by the smallest touch, the most fleeting gesture, of compassion. Whoever Akira Kurosawa is, however he came into his greatness as a film director, it was by more than knowing his lenses and his cameras. He knows how difficult it is to live, how necessary to love.

# JESSE ZUNSER

◆◇◆◇◆◇◆◇◆◇◆◇◆◇◆◇◆◇◆◇◆◇◆◇◆◇◆◇◆◇◆◇◆◇◆◇◆◇◆◇◆◇◆◇◆◇◆

The first Japanese film in fourteen years to play New York arrives, preceded by hosannas from the Venice International Film Festival, where it won the first world prize. For once, Venice seems to have been right. *Rashomon* is a symphony of sight, sound, light, and shadow, in celluloid. It is an extraordinary motion picture combination: a rarely beautiful film that forms a memorable visual setting for an absorbing drama—as brilliant in its multifaceted plot as a cut gem, as fascinating in the variety of its engrossing complexities as a chess problem, and as penetrating in its study of theoretical logic, human behavior, and playwright-plotting as any picture within recall.

*Rashomon* is one story, and five; one mystery, and many. Based on an ancient Japanese legend, it relates five differing interpretations of a solitary event: a forest bandit's attack upon a noble and his lady, the seduction of the woman, and the death of the man. The author of the age-old, fivefold drama sought to discover, through the tortuous maze of men's minds and their lies, the great and ultimate Truth. The variations on the theme include eyewitness accounts of the woodchopper who first finds the victim's body; the policeman who later captures the bandit; the ravished wife; the dead man himself, who speaks through a medium. And finally, there

*From* Cue, *December 29, 1951. Reprinted by permission of the publisher.*

is another version by the woodcutter, and a profound comment or two by a Buddhist priest.

Which story tells the truth—or even part of the truth—is left to the audience. The priest, who listens in silence to the astonishing tale on the steps of a towering, dilapidated gateway leading to the ancient capital of Kyoto, sits in a driving rain, seeking for the secret of what truly goes on in men's hearts. The priest believes that Truth —as the ultimate good that is in all men—will out. For, truly, men are, at heart, not evil; since evil is only a part—but not the whole part—of man's nature. The relating of this dramatic epic is exquisitely sensitive, cast in impressive cadences. Indeed the film itself is innately poetic, swinging in singing rhythms of mood, movement, music, and speech—merging time, space, and the eternal verities into graceful, measured, ineffably lovely photographic images. The accompanying score, although derivative, is an intriguing mixture of Occidental and Oriental offbeats.

The actors are of course unknown to America, but probably not for long: the bandit Toshiro Mifune, the woman Machiko Kyo, the husband Masayuki Mori, and the others. But it is the director, Akira Kurosawa, who takes first honors in this film drama. There have been few pictures to compare with it.


## JOHN BEAUFORT

◆◇◆◇◆◇◆◇◆◇◆◇◆◇◆◇◆◇◆◇◆◇◆◇◆◇◆◇◆◇◆◇◆◇◆◇◆◇◆◇◆◇◆◇◆


A strange tale of eighth-century Japan has come to the screen in *Rashomon*, the surprise Japanese entry which won the top award

*From* The Christian Science Monitor, *January 2, 1952.* © *copyright 1952 The Christian Science Publishing Society. All rights reserved. Reprinted by permission of the publisher.*

at last summer's Venice Film Festival. Acted in a combination of realistic and traditional styles, the film strikes a Western spectator as strangely fascinating, oddly entertaining, and on occasion powerfully affecting.

*Rashomon,* which is based on Ryunosuke Akutagawa's novel, *In the Forest,* has heretofore baffled Japanese moviemakers. Director-writer Akira Kurosawa and his brilliant cameraman, Kazuo Miyagawa, solved the story's problems with a boldly simple, essentially visual technique.

Here is the tale of a crime, retold from the viewpoints of three living witnesses and the ghost of a fourth. A firewood dealer who is out in the forest sees a bandit hold up a samurai and his wife, violate the wife, and kill the samurai. The camera's eye is used to record the conflicting versions of the crime as told by the bandit, the wife, the husband's ghost (who speaks through a medium), and the woodcutter.

The picture undoubtedly gains in impact from this repetitive technique. On the other hand, the repetition itself occasionally tends to become monotonous. The monotony is intensified by the at times heavily mannered and—by most Western standards—exaggerated style and performance.

Yet modern and traditional styles are blended more successfully than one might think possible. The realism of the duel between the bandit and the samurai, for instance, is combined with a certain stylized movement, thus heightening the total effect. (For sheer physical violence, the fight scenes match anything one might encounter in a Hollywood film.) Again, when the wife tells her version of the crime, Machiko Kyo relies heavily on the extravagant sobbing and pliant attitudinizing of traditional Japanese acting.

More than once, *Rashomon* reminds one of the material and technique of Japan's *Kabuki* theater. The figure of the medium, who tells the murdered samurai's story, is a familiar figure from Japan's classic folklore and drama.

A fable quality pervades the film; even the characters are designated simply as the Woman, the Bandit, the Man, the Firewood

Dealer, the Priest, the Medium, and the Police. But whatever elements are borrowed from the past reach the spectator through the
techniques and technology of the present.

Throughout the trial scenes, the priest and the firewood dealer
sit motionless in the background, creating a sense of visually aesthetic perspective. Yet the means of registering the scene is a wide-
angle lens with what seems an unusual depth of focus. The witnesses deliver their testimony directly in front of the camera—with
the result that the spectator finds himself in the position of judge.
It is an effective device. The episodes in the mountainous wood-
land, particularly the recurrent chases, are beautifully and excit-
ingly photographed.

The sequences at the temple—which provide the framework for
the flashback narration—are equally impressive. They are shot amid
torrential rain. And when it rains in *Rashomon,* the spectator is
treated to nothing short of a deluge. The storm during which the
firewood dealer begins his weird account finally subsides. Its end
produces the contrasting quietude, the surcease from turmoil and
torment for the good deed which restores the priest's badly shat-
tered faith in human decency and truthfulness.

*Rashomon* is set in ancient Kyoto, and the title refers to the main
gate where the story begins and ends. At the time of the action, the
city's original splendor had long since been lost, owing to natural
disasters, wars, and troublesome times. For Japanese spectators,
then, the picture may serve as an ancient fable with a modern application.

It is a question how much of this sort of exotic Oriental fare the
unaccustomed Western appetite can absorb. But *Rashomon* undoubtedly deserves attention as an authentic piece of motion picture art, a use of the medium in which traditional material emerges
fresh and vivid due to masterful and unusual employment of the
film medium.

# *ANONYMOUS*

◆◆◆◆◆◆◆◆◆◆◆◆◆◆◆◆◆◆◆◆◆◆◆◆◆◆◆◆◆◆◆◆◆◆◆◆◆◆◆◆◆◆◆◆◆◆◆◆◆◆◆◆

*Rashomon,* the first Japanese film to reach Manhattan in 14 years, is an interesting cinematic curiosity, quite unlike anything produced in the West. The judges at the 1951 Venice Film Festival gave it their Grand Prize, and other moviegoers may also be impressed by its expert photography, fluent direction, and scorching insight—in terms of peculiarly Oriental flavor—into the frailty of the human animal the world over.

A strange film even by the standards of Japan (where it drew only enough business to meet its cost of $140,000), *Rashomon* opens in a ruined eighth-century temple, where a woodcutter and a Buddhist priest, taking shelter from a lashing rain, ponder a bewildering crime that has shaken their faith in men. As they recount the crime to a cynical passerby, flashbacks picture the testimony at the trial and four differing reenactments of the violent incident itself.

Up to a point, the facts are undisputed: A bandit has stalked a traveling samurai and his wife through the forest, decoyed the husband, trussed him up, and raped the wife in his presence. Coming on the scene afterward, the woodcutter has found the samurai dead, his goods stolen.

But how and why did the husband die? In turn, the movie gives the dramatized explanations of the arrogant bandit, the tearful widow, and, through the weird incantations of a medium, the dead husband. Each of these contradictory accounts is fundamentally a lie, colored by the guilty motives of the teller. All three are exposed by a fourth version, told by the woodcutter, who turns out to have

*From* Time, *The Weekly Newsmagazine, January 7, 1952, p. 72.*
*Copyright 1952 by Time Inc. Reprinted by permission of the publisher.*

been an eyewitness to the whole incident; and even the woodcutter falsifies some of his own story to let himself off easy.

Brilliantly acted, *Rashomon* bulges with barbaric force. The bandit (Toshiro Mifune) is an unforgettable animal figure, grunting, sweating, swatting at flies that constantly light on his half-naked body, exploding in hyenalike laughter of scorn and triumph. But, more than a violent story, the film is a harsh study of universal drives stripped down to the core: lust, fear, selfishness, pride, hatred, vanity, cruelty. The woodcutter's version of the crime lays bare the meanness of man with Swiftian bitterness and contempt.

Then, as if unwilling to end on so despairing a note, Director Akira Kurosawa tacks on a hopeful epilogue: The three men in the rain-drenched ruins discover an abandoned baby, and, by the unselfish act of volunteering to adopt the child, the woodcutter restores the priest's faith in humanity. Though the film could hardly have found a better example of a compassionate saving grace, the scene seems an arbitrary afterthought that does not fit the story.

*Rashomon* has other failings. Its slow pace is deliberate and consistent enough to be accepted as a matter of style, presumably designed to the Japanese taste, yet U.S. moviegoers are likely to find much of it draggy. One long sequence is spoiled by a musical score that borrows freely from Ravel's *Boléro,* and Director Kurosawa, though obviously gifted, sometimes becomes self-consciously infatuated with the look of his own images. For all that, *Rashomon* is a novel, stimulating moviegoing experience, and a sure sign that U.S. film importers will be looking hard at Japanese pictures from now on.

# BOSLEY CROWTHER

❖◈❖◈❖◈❖◈❖◈❖◈❖◈❖◈❖◈❖◈❖◈❖◈❖◈❖◈❖◈❖◈❖◈❖◈❖◈❖◈❖

## DECEMBER 27, 1951

*Rashomon,* which created much excitement when it suddenly appeared upon the scene of the Venice Film Festival last autumn and carried off the Grand Prize, is, indeed, an artistic achievement of such distinct and exotic character that it is difficult to estimate it alongside conventional story films. On the surface, it isn't a picture of the sort that we're accustomed to at all, being simply a careful observation of a dramatic incident from four points of view, with an eye to discovering some meaning—some rationalization—in the seeming heartlessness of man.

At the start, three Japanese wanderers are sheltering themselves from the rain in the ruined gatehouse of a city. The time is many centuries ago. The country is desolate, the people disillusioned, and the three men are contemplating a brutal act that has occurred outside the city and is preying upon their minds.

It seems that a notorious bandit has waylaid a merchant and his wife. (The story is visualized in flashback, as later told by the bandit to a judge.) After tying up the merchant, the bandit rapes the wife and then—according to his story—kills the merchant in a fair duel with swords.

However, as the wife tells the story, she is so crushed by her husband's contempt after the shameful violence and after the bandit has fled that she begs her husband to kill her. When he refuses, she

From the New York Times, *December 27, 1951, and January 6, 1952.* © *1951/1952 by the New York Times Company. Reprinted by permission of the publisher.*

faints. Upon recovery, she discovers a dagger which she was holding in her hands is in his chest.

According to the dead husband's story, as told through a medium, his life is taken by his own hand when the bandit and his faithless wife flee. And, finally, a humble wood-gatherer—one of the three men reflecting on the crime—reports that he witnessed the murder and that the bandit killed the husband at the wife's behest.

At the end, the three men are no nearer an understanding than they are at the start, but some hope for man's soul is discovered in the willingness of the wood-gatherer to adopt a foundling child, despite some previous evidence that he acted selfishly in reporting the case.

As we say, the dramatic incident is singular, devoid of conventional plot, and the action may appear repetitious because of the concentration of the yarn. And yet there emerges from this picture —from this scrap of a fable from the past—a curiously agitating tension and a haunting sense of the wild impulses that move men.

Much of the power of the picture—and it unquestionably has hypnotic power—derives from the brilliance with which the camera of Director Akira Kurosawa has been used. The photography is excellent and the flow of images is expressive beyond words. Likewise the use of music and of incidental sounds is superb, and the acting of all the performers is aptly provocative.

Machiko Kyo is lovely and vital as the questionable wife, conveying in her distractions a depth of mystery, and Toshiro Mifune plays the bandit with terrifying wildness and hot brutality. Masayuki Mori is icy as the husband, and the remaining members of the cast handle their roles with the competence of people who know their jobs.

Whether this picture has pertinence to the present day—whether its dismal cynicism and its ultimate grasp at hope reflect a current disposition of people in Japan—is something we cannot tell you. But, without reservation, we can say that it is an artful and fascinating presentation of a slice of life on the screen. The Japanese dialogue is translated with English subtitles.

JANUARY 6, 1952

The unprecedented experience presented this past holiday of having a Japanese movie turn up as one of the choice films of the year has fired such amazement and interest in this particular neck of the woods that it rates an exclusive contemplation in this first screed of 1952.

*Rashomon,* the picture in question, was mentioned here briefly last week as this corner's nomination as the past year's best foreign-language film. And before that, the readers of these pages had been made acquainted with it as the out-of-the-blue Grand Prize winner at the Venice Film Festival last fall. Yet none of these notifications has fully or sufficiently conveyed the strange and disturbing fascination of this conspicuously uncommon film. And we have an uncomfortable feeling that this may turn out inadequate, too.

For the character of this picture is difficult to define because of its dissimilarity to all the familiar types of films. Where storytelling in movies is almost exclusively confined to the forward (or backward) development of a formal dramatic plot, the narrative achievement of this picture is evolved from a single episode, with this one episode—an act of violence—looked at from several points of view. And where pure emotional stimulation is the primary purpose of most films, a deep agitation of the think-box is the strange aim of *Rashomon.*

What we have here, to put it briefly, are four eyewitness accounts of an act that took place in a forest in Japan many centuries ago, brought out in the course of the musings of three wanderers reflecting upon the crime. The first account, as illustrated for the audience sitting as judge, is that of a wild and brutal bandit who precipitated the whole thing. This bandit, with characteristic bluster, tells how he cleverly waylaid an innocent city merchant traveling through the forest with his wife; how he tied up the merchant to rob him and then, overcome by lust, ravished the not reluctant woman before her husband's eyes. After this act, as he tells it, he set the husband free and fought him fairly and squarely for the possession of the now discountenanced wife. In this sword duel he killed the husband, but during it the woman fled.

This is not the wife's story, however. As she recounts the episode, she was the innocent victim of a brutal rape, and her husband's death followed as an accident when he refused to have compassion upon her. Not so in his recollection. Through a medium, the dead husband says that he made his own quietus when he saw the infidelity of his wife. And, finally, a humble woodchopper, who is one of three trying to fathom the crime, reports that he witnessed the whole thing and that it wound up in a horrible, savage fight brought on by the wife's shameless urging that the bandit kill her spouse.

After pondering this weird act of violence, the three troubled wanderers conclude that man is a frail and selfish creature. But hope is seen at the end when the woodchopper shows humanity toward an abandoned child.

As one can see, this drama—this probing of a single episode—is far from the usual order of the familiar "story" film. The incident recounted is slender, so far as material goes, and, being repeated four times, it tends, by conventional rules, to pall. Indeed, it will pall very quickly for those who are not prepared to abandon their normal expectations of plot development and suspense and find fresh and subtle stimulation in a strange, analytical approach.

For the wonderful thing about this picture—the thing which sets it up as art—is the manifest skill and intelligence with which it has been made by Director Akira Kurosawa, who moves to the top ranks with this job. Everyone seeing the picture will immediately be struck by the beauty and grace of the photography, by the deft use of forest light and shade to achieve a variety of powerful and delicate pictorial effects. Others, more attentive, will delight in the careful use of music (or absence of music) to accompany the points of view. But only the most observant—and the most sensitive—will fully perceive the clever details and devices by which the director reveals his characters, and, in this revelation, suggests the dark perversities of man.

# MANNY FARBER

◈◈◈◈◈◈◈◈◈◈◈◈◈◈◈◈◈◈◈◈◈◈◈◈◈◈◈◈◈◈◈◈◈◈◈◈◈◈◈◈◈◈◈◈◈◈◈◈◈◈

*Rashomon.* A torpid, stylish Japanese study in human frailty, like nothing so much as a tiny aquarium in which a few fish and a lot of plants have delicately been tinkered with by someone raised in Western art-cinema theaters and art galleries. Five characters, two unfrequented real-life sets—a ruined temple and a forest—and a script which is probably the first to describe a highly contrived sword-fight-and-seduction through the biased eyes of four different people. The villain is a conceited, slothful, bug-ridden bandit (Toshiro Mifune)—a type now familiar in Hollywood adventure-comedies about Mexico—who has a hard time pulling himself away from a good nap to ravish the wife of a traveling samurai. Makes its play for posterity with such carefully engineered actions as one in which the dozing barbarian scratches his crotch while the sword across his knees somehow rises (Maya Deren–fashion) as though it had just had a big meal of sex hormones. *Rashomon* is supposed to get down to the bedrock of such emotions as lust, fear, and selfishness, but actually it is a smooth and somewhat empty film whose most tiresome aspect is the slow, complacent, Louvre-conscious, waiting-for-prizes attitude of everyone who worked on it.

# JOHN McCARTEN

◆◆◆◆◆◆◆◆◆◆◆◆◆◆◆◆◆◆◆◆◆◆◆◆◆◆◆◆◆◆◆◆◆◆◆◆◆◆◆◆◆◆◆◆◆◆◆◆◆◆◆◆◆

The other day, the National Board of Review selected *Rashomon*, a Japanese film, as the best foreign picture of the year. It had previously been awarded some kind of prize at one of those European movie festivals, where accolades are passed around as casually as politicians' cigars. Lest these salutes lead you to think that yet another threat to Hollywood is looming, this time in the Orient, I feel I must tell you that *Rashomon* is a lot more simple-minded than any product of the mysterious East has any right to be, and that before it winds up, with a seedy priest and an unwashed woodsman passing an abandoned baby back and forth in the ruins of a pagoda, it has subjected us to a series of inscrutable variations on a Japanese theme involving the sort of carryings-on that stood Queens Village on its ear when Mr. Gray and Mrs. Snyder were on the loose there.

In this case, the trouble takes place in Kyoto in the eighth century. While guiding his wife through a forest close by, a travelling man (inexplicably dressed in dapper plus-fours) meets up with a bandit, who advises him that he has some hot swords hidden in a nearby glen. Although the bandit keeps jumping around and giggling, the travelling man overlooks these manifest peculiarities, on the ground that a good deal is a good deal. The bandit, however, is a sneak who hasn't any swords at all. What he wants is the travelling man's wife, and suddenly he trusses up the husband and proceeds to rape the lady. When the husband is found stabbed to death, the police have a terrible time discovering just how the deed was done. The bandit swears he did it in a fair fight; the lady says that the bandit ran away before her husband came to grief.

These accounts of the affair are given in flashbacks, which become awfully wearing, since the actors keep wheezing, grunting, gurgling, and falling down. To add to the general air of foolishness, a medium presently turns up and says she's been in touch with Daddy in the beyond. Damned if he doesn't swear he committed suicide. Somehow, all this becomes a conversation piece for the priest and woodsman I mentioned a while back, and also for another character —this one right out of *Fu-Manchu*—who has taken refuge from the rain in the ruined pagoda. When it rains in Kyoto, it really rains, and Akira Kurosawa, who directed *Rashomon*, has seen to it that everybody is half-drowned. He has also seen to it that any time his actors have a chance to give their features a thoroughgoing emotional workout, they are photographed in closeup. Perhaps I am purblind to the merits of *Rashomon*, but no matter how enlightened I may become on the art forms of Nippon, I am going to go on thinking that a Japanese potpourri of Erskine Caldwell, Stanislavski, and Harpo Marx isn't likely to provide much sound diversion.

# PIERRE MERCIER

◈◈◈◈◈◈◈◈◈◈◈◈◈◈◈◈◈◈◈◈◈◈◈◈◈◈◈◈◈◈◈◈◈◈◈◈◈◈◈◈◈◈◈◈◈◈◈

*Rashomon* was chosen by the French Federation of Ciné-Clubs as the film to be screened at its annual convention because the administrative board agreed it was an important work; moreover, it

*From* Cahiers du Cinéma, *no. 24, June 24, 1953. Reprinted by permission of Les Éditions de l'Étoile. Translated by Elliott Stein.*

probably had not been seen by many members who live in small towns.

Why then such a display of pedantry and snobbism on the part of several of the delegates? Because of this the public discussion at the *Rashomon* screening was the worst "debate" in the history of the Clermont-Ferrand Ciné-Club. Was it travel fatigue, or merely a desire to animate the discussion and provoke violent reactions? After a few of these heated exclamations, the rest of the audience just stared in silent disapproval.

Jean Faurez had given some of the film's background and proposed a study of the Japanese film in relation to other art forms. Many spectators were displeased by the unsatisfactory turn the discussion took. One of them, M. Louis, wrote to me. Here is an extract from his letter:

My disappointment at the Paris cinema the other evening was too great to keep to myself. Although I raised my hand several times, I never got to speak. Later, at home, thinking of the discussion, I mused that it would have been just as dumb to pull a flower apart to ask oneself why the stem was curved, or why, on biting into it, the taste was unpleasant. Look here, gentlemen! The *Rashomon* discussion is worthy of a satiric article which could go something like this—"Clermont-Ferrand. There was a real massacre at the Paris cinema last Thursday. With one blow, four international prizes and one (yellow) civilization were knocked out, all this caused by a film whose theme is—he who studies individual human behavior and finds it dubious can nonetheless retain his faith in humanity."

This movie does have a theme, after all. It is evident that mankind (questions of historical period, conventions, and skin color aside) has always been concerned with the same eternal human problems. One of the characters repeats, "Nowadays . . ." But the problem is eternal: Is humanity really bad? If so, why bother building, raising children, why bother living?

Questions of this nature certainly should have been brought up during the discussion. *Rashomon* does tell a story, and even the aesthetes and nit-pickers on hand might have benefited from a dialogue taking into consideration those story elements which are the opium of the normal moviegoer.

There is nothing new about *Rashomon*'s story, but its implications are for all time. These characters who lived around 700 A.D., are they even strongly situated in time in the film? In spite of costumes and swords, they are not; they do not seem terribly exotic to us. We have here the eternal theme of human degradation brought on by war. Japan has just emerged from a war.

Each of the characters reacts according to his own individual psychology, both in the drama and through his testimony in court. These character studies are not simplistic; they are precise and discreet, leaving a margin of interpretation for the spectator. Not one of the characters arouses total sympathy or antipathy. One may disapprove, even condemn—but a certain admiration for Tajomaru's vitality adds shading to the audience's opinion. Who inspires more antipathy, the bandit or the samurai? There is only one character who does strike us as despicable—the servant, whose shrewdness does not justify his cynicism.

Perhaps the film is misogynous. Masago, the woman, is certainly the most complex character, but also the most disturbing. Her ambiguity might be explained by her role as prey—of both husband and bandit. Through her sensuality she may be seen as having deep affinities to Tajomaru. Aren't the two most *alive* characters Masago and Tajomaru? Is Masago so different from the average woman?

The story, or rather the sum total of the diverse stories, does not provide us with a definite conclusion. If we do get to know those who might have wanted to kill, at the end we do not know who actually did kill. The woodcutter, the simplest and most sincere of the characters, does not furnish us a key to the enigma.

The four different versions of the drama are not presented for purely formal reasons, but correspond to the characters' differing psychic states. These versions are linked by technical means remarkable in every way—script, photography, editing, use of sound—with precise aesthetic and psychological effects in mind. The makers of *Rashomon* are obviously well-acquainted with the cinema and the classics of film history. Nothing is sloppy; the effects are tried and true, but never heavy-handed or gratuitous. It is a well-made film.

Some examples:

—The general structure, with an alternation of gate and story sequences.

—The number of actors in each shot and their placement in space. This is most evident during the police-court scenes: Masago's testimony in the foreground, with, in the background and to the right, the woodcutter and the priest. Another shot is composed of two characters in the foreground, one in back.

—Transitions from police court to forest and gate. Most striking, a dissolve during which two characters disappear from screen right as two characters reappear on the left under the gate.

—Ellipses, notably those during the police-court and rape scenes.

—Erotic symbolism used for all the characters, often for the police agent, and above all for the woman: dagger, rope, certain shapes in the ground and of objects.

—Several details in the actors' performances which reveal character with great precision: the sensual abandon of Tajomaru at the foot of the tree, the erotic way Masago's hand plays with the water, as opposed to the purity of the veil which covers her— this veil which forms a mysterious blot in the forest clearing. Masago's flat features when seen fullface are unerotic, and one is positively taken aback by the absence of eyebrows; but the same Masago, overcome by pleasure, this satanic woman seen in profile, it is she who is responsible for the drama.

—The deliberate heaviness of certain images. The scene with the woodcutter in the forest is edited with *brio*—the audience is seized by its dramatic intensity, augmented by the way the branches pass, the sun's brightness reflected in the leaves, and the pulsating progression of the musical rhythm.

—Musical counterpoint, the use of sounds: birds, cries, breathing, sobs, the sound of sawing. At times a sound provides a strange note, and a charming birdcall may reinforce the horror of the unfolding drama. In the magic scene, the voice's depersonalization reinforces the photography's grey aura. If the story takes place in a sunny cheerful landscape, the thoughts of those testifying are framed in a background where nature is disturbed.

What if the music is not Japanese? The judicious use of music by Ravel and de Falla is not irritating.

Even considering the film's faults, the FFCC did well to screen it —but it merited a less superficial debate. The moral conclusions of its Japanese *auteurs* is on a high humanistic level.

A film's form is only worthy of praise when it is adequately adapted to a content of quality. This is true of *Rashomon*.

# COMMENTARIES

# Drama and Lesson of the Defeated
## *PAOLO JACCHIA*

◆◇◆◇◆◇◆◇◆◇◆◇◆◇◆◇◆◇◆◇◆◇◆◇◆◇◆◇◆◇◆◇◆◇◆◇◆◇◆◇◆◇◆

It is not easy to attempt a complete and detailed analysis of the
Japanese film *Rashomon,* the work by Akira Kurosawa which was
recently awarded the Grand Prize at the Venice Film Festival, together with Robert Bresson's *Diary of a Country Priest,* as well as
the Italian Critics' Prize. We know almost nothing of the Japanese
cinema; we know even less of that country's contemporary culture,
and, above all, of its postwar spiritual condition. This film, in any
case, seemed to us to have a specific meaning, a particular value, in
itself. We are not referring to the director's technique, nor to problems of style; it is rather the spirit, the sense, the content of the
work, which causes us even now to meditate on it. We have per-
ceived in it the reflection of a social, spiritual, and human condition which seems to be that of an entire nation, thus assuming a
universal significance. This is a film of today, one which concerns
us directly, even though it arrives veiled in an exotic guise.

*Rashomon* takes the form of an ancient dramatic fable; and
when the drama begins to unfold, it seems to base itself on the
eternal themes of great primitive tragedy: good and evil, violence,
honor, justice, betrayal, fidelity, human respect. The central problem can be defined as the problem of truth, as posed by four interpretations of an ambiguous incident of violence; there is an element of the mystery story in it, just as there is in *Oedipus Rex.*
Who is to be believed, among the four persons, each of whom gives

*Abridged from* Bianco e Nero *12, no. 10 (October 1951). Reprinted
by permission of the publisher. Translated by Robert M. Connolly.*

his own version of the facts? Perhaps someone is lying; perhaps they are all lying. But perhaps there is also someone who is telling the truth, someone to be believed. At this point, the film poses its true problem: Can one still believe, in this world of ours?

The drama is brought to a metaphysical plane, surpassing the act of violence itself and its protagonists. These protagonists and the act itself become symbolic of a social condition, of a political situation. The scene is a postwar period in the barbaric High Middle Ages—massacres, robberies, violence of every kind are everywhere, and seemingly without end. Underlined by a chorus of three characters, this situation is the realistic premise from which Kurosawa begins his tragedy, bringing it to a metaphysical plane, at which point the original act of violence becomes, as we have said, no longer important in itself, as it would in a modern mystery story, but rather a symptomatic fact like those of the parables, of the apologues.

Gradually, as the four versions of that act of violence unfold, another drama, rising from the political situation, becomes dominant. Surrounding the chorus is the jungle, bewilderment, the extreme crisis of all human and spiritual values, of the rules of society; the life and property of man are no longer worth anything, since whim and violence reign, and man has become a beast. We see the panic, the spiritual torment of two men in that chorus in which a third character, an ignoble man, acts as counterpoint: The first of those two men—a priest, the intellectual of those times—is aware, and the other—a simple man, a woodcutter—feels that collective tragedy, and suffers, and intuits its deeper meanings. Actually both are on the same spiritual plane; in fact, it is the simple man who at the end solves the collective human and spiritual problem, indicating, with his act of faith and goodness, the way to salvation, in an atmosphere of evangelic parable.

As the interpretations of that act of violence contradict each other, an act which seems increasingly mysterious in itself but even more tragically clear inasmuch as it represents a fact of daily life of a given historical moment, the torment of the intellectual and the simple man increases. They shout, and here is the culminating point of the film—their eagerness to believe, their spiritual need to believe once more. Theirs is a spiritual exigency which goes beyond the concepts of goodness, of human respect, of charity, conceived on an interior, individual moral plane; it is a social, a collective exigency.

Their traditional religious faith is also in crisis: There is a moment in which they doubt even the truth of the words of a voice from the other world, illuminating and sacred. It is the faith of man in man, of man in the social man, which they seek; it is a need of justice, of social order, of peace. It is a profound reaction to the whim of violence, which is war; a reaction to a degeneration of man, to a disintegration of society, and to the dissolution of a patrimony of degenerated traditions, whose masks have fallen away, revealing a horrendous face, the face of a frenzied beast, in a landslide which has also swept away all the positive, human, social, and spiritual values of that society.

We see the myth of the samurai crumble for all times, degraded and defiled; the symbolic flesh and human dignity of a woman trampled upon and tormented; the unleashed bestiality of a former man who has become a wild animal with a sword, cunning, hunted, hungry for prey, and who laughs at the law; and the impiety of another man, the third member of the chorus, as degraded as the samurai, as his own ravished wife, as the woodsman who lied to the law out of fear, and as the priest who no longer believes; the wretched figure who rips off the fixtures of a temple to build a fire, to keep warm. It is the total drama of a country which is primitive, exalted, fanatical, unleashed, and savage, and which is then defeated, massacred, which not only no longer believes, but even if it wanted to, would not know what to believe in. More than Japan in defeat, the Japan of the wartime and postwar period, it is the war and the aftermath of every country which has known that tragedy; and not only the defeated countries, since violence, inhumanity, the aberrations of war infect winners and losers alike, bringing humanity and the whole of civilization to a state of crisis.

There is in the film the most profound, the most elevated, and the truest moral which a consciousness can draw from the experience of war. In our opinion, this work of Kurosawa's is more important than one which might show the physical ruins of Hiroshima; the city, in any event, can be reconstructed—just as Hitler reconstructed the Germany of Kaiser Wilhelm—whereas a civilization is reconstructed, is reborn, only when a people, having confronted those problems, acquires a conscience, and regains its own humanity. For the same reason, *Germany Year Zero,* with its tragedy of little Egmund, is more important than many German films full of ruins but devoid of conscience. In the Japanese film there is the conscience of an isolated individual, or of an advanced intellectual minority; but the dramatic, spiritual, and social exigency, which is the central theme of the film itself, is collective, surely, even though still unconscious, in that people. Vaguely symbolized by the woman —faithful and unfaithful at the same time to her man—and by the woodcutter, the Japanese people of today, with their present problems, are substantially absent from the film; if they had been present, the finale would have assumed a much vaster and more concrete meaning. In any event, despite its pathos and oversimplification and conventionality, and its mystical-religious overtones, the conclusion of *Rashomon* is a highly positive one—as is the whole of this profoundly significant new Japanese film.

# RASHOMON and the Japanese Cinema
## CURTIS HARRINGTON

◆◇◆◇◆◇◆◇◆◇◆◇◆◇◆◇◆◇◆◇◆◇◆◇◆◇◆◇◆◇◆◇◆◇◆◇◆◇◆◇◆◇◆

*Rashomon* took the Grand Prix at the Venice Festival last August to everyone's surprise, and the international fame of the film has been on the increase ever since. RKO immediately bought the American distribution rights.

*From* Cahiers du Cinéma, *no. 12 (May 1952). Reprinted by permission of* Les Éditions de l'Étoile. *Translated by Elliott Stein.*

As expected, the film made a good deal of money in New York, and probably did well in other large American cities. It recently won both the National Board of Review prize and the Oscar for the best foreign film of the year—the two most important movie awards in the United States.

This success of *Rashomon* in the United States is most interesting, for it reveals, to one who knows how to read between the lines of praise, a *reluctant* acceptance of its obvious excellence.

Snobbery will always lead Americans to admire the qualities of a French, English, even a Swedish film. But when an Oriental country like Japan, whose customs often shock Americans (as primitive and backward), makes a film which technically and artistically surpasses the best Hollywood productions, then the amazed American critics feel uneasy and seek facile explanations based on external influences. For them, *Rashomon* is a Japanese postwar film, thus its excellence must be due to the supervision and assistance supplied by the American occupiers. Nearly all the American reviews stressed "the strong Hollywood influence in the postwar period" and stated that "the Japanese public has been spoiled by the polish of American movies which their native pictures cannot easily approach."

All this is untrue. On the contrary, the Japanese cinema can boast of a rich and brilliant past, the equal of other countries which gave birth to important film industries: France, England, the United States, Germany, Italy, Russia, and Sweden. Unfortunately, only three or four Japanese films have been seen in the West during the last thirty years; the treasures of Japanese cinema will remain unknown until a means is found to bring to one of our *Cinémathèques* a great number of the best Japanese silent and sound films, so that we can accord the Japanese the place they merit in the history of world cinema.

Most good Japanese films do not have contemporary stories, but, like *Rashomon,* are set in the past. This encourages a liberty and fantasy which prevent their becoming routine.

Japanese culture is rich in legends and fantastic tales that have been freely dipped into as source matter for films. The traditional Japanese drama has strongly influenced Japanese cinema, particularly in matters concerning style, rhythm, and acting. The camera, however, was not statically tied down to the expository methods of the theatre; it was granted freedom of movement from the very beginnings of Japanese cinema. It is significant that the Japanese adopted the screenplay as a cinematographic literary form—essentially a way of thinking directly reflecting a series of physically poetic images. On occasion, the source of inspiration was a novel (as in *Rashomon*) but this only made more evident the existence of a creative tradition easily viable for the needs of the average movie.

In 1950 I saw several recent Japanese films in a movie house at Little Tokyo, a neighborhood in Los Angeles. Japanese films are shown there all year round on double-feature bills—one costume and one modern film together. The audience is composed of Southern California Japanese. The high quality of most of these films was obvious. Some of their appeal to Occidental eyes may be attributable to their exoticism; but Hindu films are just as "exotic" for us, yet most of these are of little worth.

Nearly all the Japanese films I saw were marked by a poetic sense of imagery and rhythm of a quality seen only in the very best work of a few important Western directors; in many cases this was combined with a daring and imaginative use of the medium—fast motion, slow motion, montage shots, etc.

The Japanese were certainly influenced by both American and European cinema. They eclectically borrowed the techniques and gimmicks which aided them to express the subject matter of their films. They have been at it since around 1902, and the early works were closely modeled on Western films. What matters, though, is that a careful absorption of filmic possibilities took place, so that many Japanese films, since well before the war, have been sophisticated in both style and subject matter, and technically successful.

Before examining *Rashomon* in greater detail, let me record a few items in those Japanese films seen in Los Angeles which strongly impressed me. . . .

In *Drunken Angel,* a film set in the lower depths of Tokyo, there is a dream sequence on a foggy beach in which a man finds a white coffin swept in by the tide. He opens it with an axe; a horrible caricature of himself emerges from the coffin and chases him along the shore. Later on in the same film, two men are seen fighting in a corridor whose walls have been freshly painted. During the struggle, a can of white paint spills over and the pair are transformed into macabre figures covered with the sticky white fluid. *Sanshiro Sugata* (1943), an earlier Kurosawa film, recounts a judo legend. At one point, a fighter has been thrown to the ground during combat. He lies dead in a corner of the room; a window shutter breaks loose and falls near the body, in slow motion. The tension of that moment is broken by a close-up of a screaming woman . . . a piercing cry as she discovers the corpse.

The last part of this film is among the most remarkable sequences I have ever seen: A judo combat is taking place on a high hill beaten by the wind and covered by swaying reeds. In the background, the sky is full of dark twisted clouds passing rapidly. At the beginning of the scene, the men are hidden in the grass, their movements merely indicated by sudden changes on the surface of the reeds. It starts to rain; the reeds are flattened out by the rain—the opponents become clearly visible. Finally, the older man loses footing. Vanquished, he slips down the wet reeds, falls to his death in a ravine.

In all these films, visual poetry is the common element—a keen sense of the cinema's creative possibilities.

These tales do not become stereotyped adaptations for the screen, but are true creations in which camera, actors, sets, and music are combined in a stylized whole. Even in *Drunken Angel*, a modern gangster story set in Tokyo, there is no attempt to borrow from Italian "neorealism"; instead, we have a careful combination of all the elements to obtain certain effects. Another surprise is the great technical quality, especially that of the camera work. . . .

In *Rashomon*, Kurosawa attains a degree of camera mobility perhaps not seen since the "flying cameras" of the U.F.A. period (e.g., *Variety, The Last Laugh*).

The camera achieves a new kind of intimacy—it is so precise in its explorations, so active in its participation in the story, and yet so psychologically exact that although, critically, we may speak of a tour de force, we don't see it—we have been taken in and have become accomplices. The three principal performances work well together; the skill with which different aspects of the characters are presented as we see the story from various points of view is such that it is licit to speak of this film as veritable revelation.

It is unlikely that any Western actor would be capable of the dynamism of Toshiro Mifune's performance as the bandit, a portrait of extraordinary erotic savagery, overflowing with force and vitality.

The film's three main settings each have a dominant style distinguishing them from the others according to the humors of the scenes taking place. Thus, the temple (the main gate of the city of Kyoto) is grey, bathed in a heavy, monotonous rain; the police court, where the confession is made, is photographed in static shots in a courtyard lit by bright sun; the forest where the drama breaks out (thrice in the imagination, once in reality) is seen in a constantly changing light filtered by the leaves, which results in broad daylight in some shots and chiaroscuro in others.

The first three main episodes are accompanied by a musical theme a bit irritating to Western ears (a bolero akin to Ravel's), whereas the fourth episode—deliberately, for it is the final part that is the true story—is accompanied only by natural sounds.

It is interesting to note that the "Westernizing" musical scores in Japanese films are stylistically largely derived from French Impressionist and Postimpressionist music—Debussy, Ravel, Roussel, etc.

The novel from which the script is adapted is the work of a well-known modern writer, often called "the Japanese Hemingway." He committed suicide in 1927, after having declared himself incapable of enduring the moral problems of twentieth-century life. The construction of the story itself—the conflict between truth and untruth —is similar to that of certain plays by Pirandello.

I have not read the novel and am incapable of commenting on any changes the script writers saw fit to make. Whatever they are, the film works beautifully; it is the sort of movie which makes clear to us the freshness and the unique magic of the cinema as a means of artistic expression.

Perhaps *Rashomon*'s success abroad will finally lead to the recognition of the Japanese cinema as one of the world's great national film industries.

# RASHOMON and the Fifth Witness
## GEORGE BARBAROW

◆◆◆◆◆◆◆◆◆◆◆◆◆◆◆◆◆◆◆◆◆◆◆◆◆◆◆◆◆◆◆◆◆◆◆◆◆◆◆◆◆◆◆◆◆◆◆◆◆◆◆

*Rashomon* is rich as a fruit cake visually, and as nutty in structure. Unevenness, imbalance, and wild chaos characterize it; raucous humor is preceded in it by sensuous beauty and followed by deadly serious hysteria; theatrical scenes are placed side by side with bits of pure cinema; at some moments it is a brilliant whodunit, at others a formless philosophical tract; at its end, this prize-winning Japanese extravaganza is indistinguishable from any of a thousand Sunday School plays available at small fee from Samuel French. But after the beginning and before the end, and even during parts of these parts, *Rashomon* is what all movies ought to be as a minimum requirement for mere existence: It is unashamedly photographic, and so it deserves, these days, the loud acclaim and the popularity it has gained. Kurosawa, the director, takes delight in camera images, and fills ninety minutes of screen time with them. Some are graceful, some sentimental, some abstract, some crude and powerful, some ugly, some sensational, some conventionally dull as the *National Geographic*. But no spectator dares close his eyes once Kurosawa has established his main interest in visual images, for to turn away for one moment would be to risk losing some of the priceless pleasure of motion pictures.

The film begins with a veritable deluge of a rainstorm of such photogenic cascadence that one can hardly recollect wetter water; there follows shortly an excursion into a forest, by swiftly moving camera, that reveals interlaced dizzy patterns of branches, trunks, brush, and blazing splotches of sunlight. In the forest, there is a truly cinematic encounter of a man and his wife with a bandit, ending in a three-way duel, the conflict being described in four different ways, each purporting to be the account of a different person. The bandit's narration, the longest because it includes the encounter along the forest road, is followed by the wife's version, the husband's, and at last by a woodcutter's story. Interlarded among these highly colored, contradictory, and hence nearly incredible expositions are scenes of verbal argument and explanation at the police station, and further scenes (during the rainstorm) on the porch of an artistic-looking, half-ruined building, where the woodcutter, a tramp, and a priest discuss What It All Means.

The final and overriding complication is Kurosawa's rampaging camera, essentially a pointless instrument because it points too easily everywhere and anywhere. It is an often brilliant but always unreliable fifth witness that observes each of the others as he talks and as he acts in his own version of the desperate, passionate, and violent episode in the forest. There can be no question of accepting the testimony of the official witnesses, for Kurosawa—like Shaw, Pirandello, Gide, or Sascha Guitry—constantly makes observations that belie the "natural" development of the story, that emphasize the process of the telling in a self-conscious and often irritating manner. These observations are usually photographic: the way the pompous policeman plops into the water, the better to observe at a slightly frightened distance the groaning bandit on the river bank; the way the bandit scratches hurriedly at a louse bite during a deadly sword fight; and the way the medium does too much rolling around on the ground at the expense of more views of the husband preparing himself for suicide. What interests the director in this picture is evidently the employment of whatever good idea he happens to think of, and these improvisations are tossed in without much regard for the entire pattern of the film. Indeed, the picture's pattern is merely fortuitous. Unforgivably theatrical scenes are relieved only by the director's photographic penchant; too much is told verbally; and the panning and traveling shots in the forest, although sensuously pretty, do not clarify the structure of the whole film, and bear not the slightest relation to the theme of the picture, which is moral anarchy.

The theme has been explained very well, much better than the moviemakers have done it, by Parker Tyler, in his essay *How to Solve the Mystery of "Rashomon,"* a pamphlet recently published by Cinema 16, the film society. Mr. Tyler's main point is that the paralyzing shock of the terrifying episode in the forest accounts for the variations in the four narratives by the human witnesses. Each, in a numbed state, struggles to reestablish his own identity and, talking from his emotions, invents a story, not particularly caring whether or not it fits the facts or another's version of them. It follows that all apparent inconsistencies in *Rashomon* are actually consistent, and that the film is a "masterpiece." Mr. Tyler's encomium is ingenious and unabashed, as unabashed as Kurosawa's enthusiasm for his camera. But a masterpiece of a film is not confused and not confusing, as *Rashomon* is. It does not, and should not, like *Rashomon,* imitate in a protean manner the anarchy it proposes to reveal. A film ought not to be a hodgepodge or a ragbag, a veritable anthology of narrative styles, especially when the director possesses the fifth witness and does not fully control it. That he does not control it all the time is plain enough from the opening title and from the priest's opening speech: The events to be shown take place in a time of wars, fires, famines, earthquakes, typhoons, a time of death and destruction, hence also a time of moral decay. This stuff is verbal, and verbal stuff carries small conviction on the screen. There should be and could be better evidence that this is a time of disasters, a time when the unnatural becomes natural, when the cultural and social order is shaken to the center. What is needed in the film is cinematic evidence having the cogency of the dramatic evidence in the wonderfully articulate beginnings of *Macbeth* and *Hamlet.* It is all very well to start with an excellent rainstorm, but rain is not an earthquake and a sword fight is not a war, and a moviemaker who must rely on a direct title to make a main point is not a master.

The baby is the worst. At the end, the woodcutter is caught in a lie about his version of the forest episode. The tramp sneers. The priest feels more pain, since his faith in man is already badly damaged. Then a baby's cry is heard. It is a foundling. The tramp steals the baby's rich bedding and then leaves, as he denounces the hypocritical woodcutter for attempting to stop the theft. The latter worthy attempts to take the baby, is rebuffed by he horrified priest, then gets the baby by declaring he will bring it up as one of his own children. The priest having regained his faith, and the bathos having been multiplied unconscionably, the rain stops; and so the picture ends in a cliché so wild that Broadway audiences were able to recognize it as a joke in *Boy Meets Girl: My Gawd!, cries the grizzled prospector as he stumbles over something soft in the snow. My Gawd! A Baby!* Mr. Tyler, embarrassed by the baby, believes "the film would have remained intact without it," but we might ask how the film could have ended much differently, since the theme is expressed not by the action and visual structure of the picture but by a number of stiff and dull verbalisms of the *c'est la guerre* variety.

Such misfortunes reduce the very real pleasure and intense excitement generated by portions of *Rashomon* where sights and actions escape the inhibitions of playlet forms, but they cannot completely destroy the vitality of Kurosawa's shots. Even the slowest of "message" scenes can be sat through just by studying the compositional patterns on the screen. And when a sequence is going strong, as in the two sword fights, which are meant to be compared one with the other, the work is magnificent.

·•❦ ESSAYS ❧•·

# RASHOMON
## by DONALD RICHIE

Kurosawa had for some time wanted to make the film that eventually became *Rashomon*. A scenario was written, a budget was determined, and then (in 1948) the picture was cancelled because the small Toyoko Company, which was to have financed it, decided it was too much of a risk. Toho—Kurosawa's company off and on for a number of years—was against it. Then Daiei signed a one-year distribution and production contract with Kurosawa. He and his associates left Toho to form the short-lived Motion Picture Art Association, and one of the director's hopes was to be able to make this picture.

After making *Scandal*, Kurosawa showed Daiei the script which became *Rashomon*. "It was a bit too short . . . but all of my friends liked it very much. Daiei, however, did not understand it and kept asking: But what is it about? I made it longer, put on a beginning and an ending—and they eventually agreed to make it. Thus Daiei joined those—Shochiku for *The Idiot,* Toho for *Record of a Living Being*—who were brave enough to try something different." This is a very charitable statement. Actually Daiei was adamant in its refusal to understand. Masaichi Nagata, head of the studio and standing somewhat in relation to Japanese film as Darryl Zanuck once stood to American production, walked out on the first screening and, until the picture began winning prizes abroad, was very fond of telling the press how little he understood *his* film—his,

*From* The Films of Akira Kurosawa, *2nd ed., by Donald Richie (Berkeley and Cambridge: University of California Press, 1970), pp. 70–80. Reprinted by permission of the Regents of the University of California.*

since he, in the manner of a Goldwyn or a Zanuck, or a Wald, often signs his own name as executive producer. Toho never gave adequate foreign distribution to *Record of a Living Being* and Shochiku butchered *The Idiot.*

The beginnings of *Rashomon* lie in the stories of Ryunosuke Akutagawa, that brilliant and erratic stylist who died, a suicide of thirty-five, in 1927. His position in Japanese letters, although secure, has always been special—as special as that of Poe in America or Maupassant in France. He has always been extremely popular and also critically well thought of almost despite his popularity. Yet he has never been considered in the "mainstream" of Japanese literature. His defenders point out his inventive style; his detractors call him "Western" in his orientation. He *is* "Western" in the same way as Kurosawa: He is concerned with truths which are ordinarily outside pragmatic Japanese morality and, being concerned with them, he questions them. This he does with an involuted, elliptical style, the essence of which is irony. In translation he sounds very *fin de siècle,* a better Beardsley, a less-involved Lafcadio Hearn—although there is no trace of this in Kurosawa's film.

It is based, loosely, upon two of Akutagawa's hundred-odd short stories: the title story, *Rashomon,* and *In a Grove*—which gives the film its plot, or plots. The title story has little in it that Kurosawa used, except the general description of the ruined gate, the conversation about the devastation of Kyoto during the period of civil wars, and the atmosphere of complete desolation. The story, like the film, begins in the rain. A discharged servant shelters himself under the gate, then decides to wait in the loft for the weather to clear. There he finds an old woman who is stealing hair from the corpses left there. She pleads that she only steals to make a living by making wigs from the stolen hair. The servant, who has decided to become a thief, knocks her down and takes her clothes, saying that her defense has proved his own. He runs away and that is the end of the story.

*In a Grove* opens abruptly with the testimony of a woodcutter before the police. This is followed by various testimonies: that of a priest, a police agent, an old woman who turns out to be the mother of the girl the bandit raped, the bandit himself, the girl herself, the murdered man through a medium, and there is no conclusion; the reader is presented with seven testimonies and given no indication of how he should think about them. Akutagawa's point was the simple one that all truth is relative, with the corollary that there is thus no truth at all.

Kurosawa's most significant addition (besides that of the abandoned baby in the last scenes) is the introduction of the character of the commoner, a cynical yet inquisitive man, whose questions and disbelief act as a comment upon all the various versions of the story. The commoner talks to both priest and woodcutter—since all three are found under the gate at the beginning of the film—and in a way acts as a moral (or amoral) chorus. He is the single person in the cast of eight (the medium herself is involved because she speaks for the dead man) who is essentially uninvolved. He alone has no story, no version to tell. It is through his questions that the film evolves.

First the woodcutter tells how he went into the forest and found the woman's hat, some rope, an amulet case, and then went to the police. There he recounts how he found the body. The priest's testimony follows directly. He tells how he saw the murdered man and his wife some time before. This is followed directly by the story of the police agent, who tells how he managed to capture the bandit. His story is broken into by the bandit, who tells the apparent truth of his capture and continues to give the first version of the tragedy.

He was asleep under a tree when the man and wife went past; the wind blew her veil and he saw her and decided he wanted her. He tricked the husband into following him, tied him up, went back, got the wife, raped her in front of the husband, and then turned to go when she stopped him, saying that her honor demanded that they fight. In the resulting duel the bandit killed the husband and the woman ran away.

The second version is the woman's in the police court. She takes up the story after the rape, says that the bandit went away and that her own husband spurned her because she had been (presumably so easily) violated. Wild with grief, she apparently kills him, then runs away and is finally found by the police.

The third version is that of the dead husband himself, speaking through the lips of a medium. He says that after the rape the bandit made overtures, wanting to take her away with him. She agrees and then insists that he kill the husband. This angers the bandit, who spurns her and goes away. The man finds the woman's dagger (which has been mentioned in all earlier versions of the story) and kills himself. Much later, after he has been dead for some time, he feels someone taking the dagger away.

The fourth version is that of the woodcutter who is prevailed upon to correct his first story. He says that after the rape he found the bandit on his knees before the woman, pleading with her to go away with him. The woman says that she cannot decide, that only the men can. They are reluctant, but she insists. They fight and the bandit kills the husband. She runs away and eventually the bandit also leaves. The woodcutter—whose own veracity is questioned when it transpires that *he* might have stolen the dagger, either from the ground or from the chest of the dead man—says, "I don't understand any of them—they don't make sense." To which the commoner replies, "Well, don't worry about it—it isn't as though men were reasonable."

This is more or less the point of the Akutagawa story and this is where the original stops. Kurosawa, however, goes on. Having invented the character of the commoner, having chosen to frame all of his stories within the general story of the three conversing under the ruined gate, he now invents a further incident. They hear a baby crying and the commoner finds it. He takes its clothes (a suggestion perhaps from the original *Rashomon* story), an act which horrifies the other two and which, in turn, makes him culpable. Throughout the picture he has not once acted, merely asked questions—now he acts and his act is immoral. The woodcutter picks up the naked child, saying he will take it home. The priest says that this single act has restored his faith in men, and the picture concludes with the rain stopping, the sun breaking through, and the woodcutter going off with the baby.

Akutagawa is content to question all moral values, all truth. Kurosawa, obviously, is not. Neither anarchist nor misanthrope, he insists upon hope, upon the possibility of gratuitous action. Like the priest, he cannot believe that men are evil—and, indeed, if Kurosawa has a spokesman in the film it is probably the priest: weak, confused, but ultimately trusting.

There is, however, much more to the film than this. There is an apparent mystery, an elliptical intent, which has fascinated audiences all over the world. Daiei was quite right to ask what the picture was about, although its dismissal of the picture as being a kind of mystification was ill-judged. One of the most fascinating aspects of the film is just that it is extremely difficult to determine *what* it means. It shares with other modern art (abstract painting, free-form sculpture) an apparent lack of ostensible meaning which (in painting) returns to us our ability to see form and color, which (in sculpture) gives us our original vision—that of children—and lets us observe rock as rock, wood as wood, and which (in films such as *Rashomon, Muriel, Paris nous appartient*) allows us to examine human action undistracted by plot, undisturbed by ostensible reality.

The central section of *Rashomon* is an anecdote presented four times, in four different ways. Each member of the triangle (bandit, woman, husband) tells his version, and the fourth is that of the only witness: the woodcutter.

At first he says only that he found the body of the husband but at the end he confesses that he saw the entire thing. Thus, it is he who might be lying. He is the only eye witness—that is, we hear the testimony of the other three only through the priest and himself, both of whom were present at the prison questioning. We never once see the others directly. Everything is history—and the story is told by the two to a third, the commoner. Further, the only link between these two sets of three people is the woodcutter himself. The husband is dead, wife and bandit are either in jail or executed for murder. In any case, all are unavailable to us. The priest only knows what he has heard wife, bandit, and husband say. So, it comes down to the woodcutter. He is the only one who saw anything. He lied once. He may lie again.

There is a further difficulty in that we are never quite certain *who* is telling some of these apparently varying stories. A breakdown of the various recountings of the anecdote gives:

| | | |
|---|---|---|
| 1. The discovery of the body. | | Told by the woodcutter. |
| 2. Man and wife seen in the forest. | | Told by the priest. |
| 3. Tajomaru's capture. | Told by the police agent. | |
| 4. Tajomaru's version of the story. | Told by Tajomaru, the bandit. | |
| 5. The wife's version. | Told by the wife. | |
| 6. The husband's version. | Told by the husband through the medium. | |
| 7. The woodcutter's version. | | Told by the woodcutter. |

The only first-person stories are therefore those of the woodcutter and the priest, and the latter only happened to see the two of them (alive) in the woods. This means that he saw them before the time of the anecdote and before the woodcutter says he saw them. That his story and the woodcutter's agree means little, since the priest actually saw nothing of the action that followed. However, it is presumed that the third-person recountings (the versions of Tajomaru, the wife, and the husband) are to be accepted as substantially true, because in the court scenes we see the woodcutter and the priest kneeling in the background and listening. Thus they have been there to hear what the three have said, and if there were any differences in this third-person version they give the commoner, one might be expected to contradict the other. This, however, must be inferred by the viewer, and given the character of the priest, it is not at all certain that he is the kind of person who would contradict even if he saw that the stories were being falsified by the woodcutter in the retelling.

To say this, however, is to presume that it is the woodcutter who is doing the retelling, and this is by no means certain. It could equally well be the priest who is recounting—or it could be both of them. Since these three stories are mutually contradictory (or at least seem to be), we are initially given the choice of disbelieving the priest and the woodcutter, or disbelieving one and/or all of the original triangle of bandit, husband, wife.

Kurosawa gives us no reason at all for disbelieving the priest. At the same time we are given very little for disbelieving what is said by any of the original three, because their stories, if lies, are not the kind of lies which one tells to escape punishment, and this would seem to be the usual reason for lying. The bandit admits to killing the husband; the wife admits to killing the husband; the husband admits to killing himself. There is no shifting of blame. Each pleads guilty.

There is, on the other hand, a reason for the woodcutter's lying. He is the only person who has something to gain from falsehood. First, as he says, he did not want to become involved with the police (then as now a dangerous alternative in Japan); second, it transpires that he might be a thief (the dagger) as well. One might understand his lying to keep clear of the police, but under the gate with an all-forgiving priest and the kind of man who steals clothes from abandoned infants, there seems little motivation for falsehood. If he stole the dagger, the other two could not care less—although the commoner might covet it.

It would seem that someone—more than one—is lying. Yet there is no reason. At this point the thought occurs: Is it not possible that no one is lying and that the stories can be reconciled?

The disagreement in the stories is only over the murder. All the stories of attack and rape agree. Kurosawa helps us very little in sorting out the different versions and their possible agreement, but he does help some. The bandit, for example, says that they fought because she insisted, and at the end of his version he backs the husband into a thicket and kills him. The woodcutter agrees with the bandit: They fought because she insisted. At the end of his version, Kurosawa is careful to show us that it is the same thicket into which the husband is backed and killed. There are many differences (emotion, intention) but the actions in the first and fourth versions agree.

The problem becomes one of having to reconcile the other two. The third version, that of the husband, may be hastily disposed of. He is dead. The dead do not speak—through the mouths of me-

diums or otherwise. That the three under the gate happen to believe
in spirits does not mean that we must. Rape, murder, these are physical facts; the talking dead are not. The poor demented woman
called upon by the magistrates, obviously terrified by her position,
makes up her own version, which (although she may believe it) is
not, *cannot* be true. (That one need not be so cavalier with both an
important section of the film and Kurosawa's express intentions
will be demonstrated later: There is perfectly good reason for be-
lieving in both the speaking dead and the veracity of the husband.)

This leaves the story of the wife. Hers is more difficult to reconcile, but not impossible (if you cheat a bit). Apparently, after the
rape, there was a lapse of some time—recounted in the woodcutter's
story as well—when the bandit was not there. During this time her
husband shows her how he has come to hate her. (This point is
agreed upon in all the stories—leaving out the husband's, which
we, for the present, have agreed is no story at all. The implication
in both the woodcutter's and the bandit's version is that it was she
who suggested the duel, and so some amount of hate between the
spouses is necessary.) She remembers that he looked at her with the
greatest scorn. She cuts his bonds, offers him her dagger, asks him
to kill her, then faints. When she revives, her husband is dead and
the dagger is in his chest.

Now, if only it were not for the dagger, all the stories would more
or less agree, because she could just as easily have either fainted or
lost her reason during a duel which followed and of which she
would have known nothing. However, the dagger remains (as well
as a number of other loose ends). Further, at the end of the film it
transpires that the woodcutter might have taken it. He has now a
very good reason for lying. Not only may he have stolen the dagger,
he might also have crept up during the wife's swoon and stabbed
the husband himself. Leaving aside the extreme unlikelihood of a
simple woodcutter daring to stab a noble, however, what would
have been the motivation for such an act? Robbery? But then a
number of their belongings would be missing, and the police do not
mention this, nor does the wife. The only missing objects are the
horse and sword (which the bandit took) and the dagger (which the
woodcutter might have taken). But let us presume that this is what

happened—that either the wife or the woodcutter killed the husband.

One can do this because the woodcutter now has a reason for lying (possible murder) and this makes his story (both parts of it) falsehood. Then one remembers that his version happened to jibe particularly well with that of the bandit. Where is the bandit now? His head has probably been cut off. At any rate he can tell us no more than the husband could. And who told us the bandit's story? Why, the woodcutter, of course. And he lied about it, even taking care that it match and thus lend credulity to his own. If he has been the one who has told us all these stories, then they are all lies. But in that case, why include two (husband's and wife's) that would weaken his own case? Perhaps it is because the priest tells some and the priest (although he has perhaps heard the bandit's story) does not presume to correct. Then, one solution to *The Great Rashomon Murder Mystery* would be:

| | | |
|---|---|---|
| 1. The discovery of the husband's body. | | A lie told by the woodcutter. |
| 2. Man and wife seen in the forest. | | The truth told by the priest. |
| 3. Tajomaru's capture. | Told by the police agent. | The truth told by the woodcutter or the priest. |
| 4. Tajomaru's version of the story. | Told by Tajomaru. | A lie told by the woodcutter. |
| 5. The wife's version. | Told by the wife. | The truth told by the priest. |
| 6. The husband's version. | Told by the husband through the medium. | Accepted as true and told by the priest. |
| 7. The woodcutter's version. | | A lie told by the woodcutter. |

There is some (not much) reason for the validity of this arrangement given in the context of the film itself. At the end of 4, the commoner is speaking to the woodcutter—as though he were re-

sponding to something which the woodcutter had told him. He says
that he thinks Tajomaru probably killed the woman as well.

*Priest:* But this woman turned up at prison too, you know. It
seems she went to seek refuge at some temple and the police found
her there.

*Woodcutter (Breaking in):* It's a lie. They're all lies. Tajomaru's
confession, the woman's story. They're lies.

*Commoner:* Well, men are only men. That's why they lie. They
can't tell the truth. Not even to each other.

*Priest:* That may be true. But it is because men are so weak.
That's why they lie. That's why they must deceive themselves.

*Commoner:* Not another sermon. I don't mind a lie—not if it's an
interesting one. What kind of story did she tell?

*Priest:* Well, hers was a completely different story from the bandit's. And, speaking of differences—the bandit talked about her
temper. I saw nothing like that at all. I found her very pitiful.
I felt a great compassion for her.

Then follows the wife's version, which, in this context, seems very
much as though retold by the priest, who, having no reason for lying, would himself tell the truth as he heard it.

It would be convenient if, at the end of 5, the woodcutter had
again said it was a lie, but he unfortunately does not. He says nothing, merely states that the next story, the husband's story, is a lie.
There is here no indication as to who tells 6, because the last word
before it begins belongs to the commoner. Besides, at that moment
(perhaps to prepare for the supernatural to come), there is a great
flash of lightning, followed by thunder. At the end of 6, the woodcutter is walking about and then stops and says that it wasn't true.
If he had been telling the dead husband's story he would not have
said this. It must have been the priest. He goes on to say that it
wasn't a dagger that killed him anyway. It was a sword. Now, we
know that the bandit stole and sold the sword, but we do actually
know how the husband was killed. The woodcutter is telling us.
Since he has lied about the dagger, there is no reason to believe this
remark about the sword. And it is here that the priest decides he

doesn't want to hear any more—almost as though he can no longer countenance such lying from the woodcutter. It is now revealed that his having said he found the body was a lie, and even the commoner becomes suspicious. At the end of 7:

*Commoner:* And I suppose that that is supposed to be true.

*Woodcutter:* I don't tell lies. I saw it with my own eyes.

*Commoner:* That I doubt.

*Woodcutter:* I don't tell lies.

*Commoner:* Well, that is just what you'd say, isn't it?—no one tells lies after he has *said* he is going to tell one.

*Priest:* It's horrible—if men do not tell the truth, do not trust one another, then the earth becomes hell indeed.

*Commoner:* Absolutely right. The world we live in is hell.

It might be assumed, then, the woodcutter is consistently lying, that the priest knows it but for some reason (fear, compassion) restrains himself. Therefore the only correct version is the woman's—which is given by the priest. Further, the woodcutter may have murdered the husband as well. The commoner says: "You say you don't lie. That's funny. You may have fooled the police but you don't fool me." Then the woodcutter attacks the commoner—perhaps not the act of an innocent man—and the two fight. Then:

*Priest (Seeing the woodcutter pick up the baby and misinter-preting his intentions):* What are you doing—trying to take what little it has left?

*Woodcutter:* I have six children of my own. One more won't make it any more difficult.

*Priest:* I'm sorry. I shouldn't have said that.

*Woodcutter:* Oh, one cannot afford not to be suspicious of people. I'm the one who is ashamed. I don't know why I did a thing like that.

A thing like what? Is he confessing, indicating his guilt to this priest who refused to expose his lies in front of the commoner? Is this a kind of covenant between the two? Then this final gesture, the saving of the baby, might be a mark of contrition. The woodcutter will save a life and make amends for the life he either himself took or else did not prevent the wife from taking. And if this is true, the final dialogue in the film is double-edged and profoundly ironic.

*Priest:* I am grateful to you. Because . . . thanks to you, I think I will be able to keep my faith in men.

But what if it were the priest who had told Tajomaru's story? What then? Well—what then indeed? The question, like this murder-mystery aspect of the film, is really irrelevant. It is only meaningful if one thinks that the picture is about relative truth. And if that were what it is about, would not Kurosawa have made the stories a bit less reconcilable than they are? If the film is about relative truth (which on one level it is, to be sure), then it is also a partial failure, because, judging merely by externals—who did what to whom—the actions are not enough at variance to make a point which one might suppose that he (like Akutagawa) was making.

One doubts very much that Kurosawa was deeply interested in objective truth in this or in any other film. This is because the *why* is always implied. And in none of his pictures is Kurosawa even slightly interested in the why of a matter. Instead, always, *how*. This offers a clue. The level of objective truth is not the truly interesting one. Much more interesting is the level of subjective truth. If the truth searched for becomes subjective, then no one lies, and the stories are wildly at variance.

Truth as it appears to others. This is one of the themes, perhaps the main one, of this picture. No one—priest, woodcutter, husband, bandit, medium—lied. They all told the story the way they saw it, the way they believed it, and they all told the truth. Kurosawa therefore does not question truth. He questions reality.

Once asked why he thought that *Rashomon* had become so popular, both in Japan and abroad, he answered, "Well, you see . . . it's about this rape." Everyone laughed, but the answer is not, perhaps, so cynical as it sounds. *Rathomon* is *about* an action as few pictures are *about* anything at all. We can turn the object this way

and that, look at it from various angles, and it resembles a number
of things but *is* only one thing, the object that it is. The film is
about a rape (and a murder), but, more than this, it is about the
reality of these events. Precisely, it is about what five people think
this reality consists of. How a thing happens may reflect nothing
about the thing itself, but it must reflect something about the person involved in the happening and supplying the *how*.

Five people interpret an action and each interpretation is different, because, in the telling and in the retelling, the people reveal
not the action but themselves. This is why Kurosawa could leave
the plot, insofar as there is one, dangling and unresolved. The fact
that it *is* unresolved is itself one of the meanings of the film.

In all of Kurosawa's pictures there is this preoccupation with the
conflict between illusion (the reactions of the five and their stories)
and reality (the fact of the rape and murder). To do something is to
realize that it is far different from what one had thought. To have
done something and then to explain it completes the cycle, because
this too is (equally) different from what the thing itself was. Given
a traumatic experience, one fraught with emotional connotations
(murder, falling in love, bankruptcy, rape), reality escapes even
more swiftly.

One can now assign various reasons for the five having seen and
heard the things that they thought they saw and heard. All the
stories have in common one single element—pride. Tajomaru is
proud to have raped and fought and killed; the wife is proud to
have (perhaps) killed; the husband (for now there is every reason
to believe that the dead talk) is proud to have killed himself; and
the woodcutter is proud to have seen and robbed. They are proud
of these actions and we know because they insist upon them. One
confesses only what one is openly or secretly proud of, which is the
reason that contrition is rarely sincere. But the reasons for the
pride, as Parker Tyler has indicated in his fine analysis of this film,
are not those commonly encountered.

Each is proud of what he did because, as he might tell you, "It is
just the sort of thing that I would do." Each thinks of his character
as being fully formed, of being a *thing*, as the rape or the dagger
is a thing, and of his therefore (during an emergency such as this)

being capable of only a certain number of (consistent) reactions.
They are *in character* because they have defined their own character
for themselves and will admit none of the surprising opportunities
which must occur when one does not. They "had no choice"; circumstances "forced" their various actions; what each did "could not
be helped." It is no wonder that the reported actions refuse to agree
with each other. As the commoner has wisely remarked, "Men are
only men . . . they can't tell the truth—not even to each other."
One of the points of the picture, then, is not that men will not but
that men *cannot* tell the truth. The priest sees this: "It is because
men are so weak. That's why they lie. That's why they must deceive
themselves."

If one is going to agree that one is a certain kind of person, one
also agrees that one is engaged in self-deception, in bad faith. We
know what Kurosawa thinks about this. From *Sugata* on, his vil-
lains have been in bad faith; that is, they see themselves as a kind
of person to whom only certain actions, certain alternatives are
open. In the effort to create themselves, they only codify; in the
effort to free themselves (by making action simpler and therefore
easier), they limit themselves.

It is interesting that *Rashomon* should have been a historical film
—Kurosawa's second (since the Japanese tend to think of the Meiji
period—the era of *Sanshiro Sugata*—as being somehow modern)—
because this limitation of spirit, this tacit agreement (social in its
scope) that one *is* and cannot become, is one feudalistic precept
which plagues the country to this day. This was as useful to the
Kamakura government as it proved to the administration during
the last war. In *Rashomon,* as in *They Who Step on the Tiger's Tail*
and *Sanjuro,* Kurosawa is presenting an indictment of feudal remains. That he sets the scene in the Heian period is merely due to
Akutagawa's having used it, and where the director follows the
author in this film, he does so literally. The people and their way of
thinking are—twelfth century or present day—completely feudal.
It is as though in this film he is holding up a mirror.

In more ways than one. *Rashomon* is like a vast distorting mirror or, better, a collection of prisms that reflect and refract reality.
By showing us its various interpretations (perhaps the husband

really loved his wife, was lost without her, and hence felt he must
kill himself; perhaps she really thought to save her husband by a
show of affection for the bandit, and thus played the role of faithful
wife; perhaps the woodcutter knows much more, perhaps he too
entered the action—mirrors within mirrors, each intention bringing
forth another, until the triangle fades into the distance), he has
shown first that human beings are incapable of judging reality,
much less truth, and second, that they must continually deceive
themselves if they are to remain true to the ideas of themselves that
they have.

Here then, more than in any other single film, is found Kurosawa's central theme: The world is illusion, you yourself make reality, but this reality undoes you if you submit to being limited by
what you have made. The important corollary—you are not, however, truly subject to this reality, you can break free from it, can
live even closer to the nature you are continually creating—this occurs only in the later films. . . .

The visual starting point remains the Akutagawa stories. The
author's description of the gate and medieval Kyoto is literally followed by both the script and camera. There is, for example, no reason at all for the bandit to be discovered by the police agent near a
small bridge (seen in the film) except that this is where Akutagawa
says it happened. What turned out to be an excellent cinematic device—all the testimonies being given to the audience, questions answered by unheard questions being repeated as a question and then
answered by those testifying—is taken directly from the author.
Likewise, in the original script, all the characters' names are re-
tained even though, in the case of husband and wife, they never
appear in the dialogue. Given the eventual difference between story
and film—which is extreme and which the Japanese critics complained of when they said the director had been false to the spirit
of the tales—such literal fidelity is remarkable.

The acting style, however, owes nothing at all to Akutagawa or
any of his suggestions. It springs from a different source. "We were
staying in Kyoto," says Kurosawa, "waiting for the set to be finished.
While we were there we ran off some 16-mm. prints to amuse our-

selves. One of them was a Martin Johnson jungle film in which there was a shot of a lion roaming around. I noticed it and told Mifune that that was just what I wanted him to be. At the same time Mori had seen a jungle picture in which a black leopard was shown. We all went to see it. When the leopard came on Machiko was so upset that she hid her face. I saw and recognized the gesture. It was just what I wanted for the young wife."

Cinematically the style is made of various parts, all of which work admirably together. Perhaps the most noticeable is a kind of rhapsodic impressionism which from time to time carries the story and creates the atmosphere. Take, for example, the much-admired walk of the woodcutter through the forest. This is pure cinema impressionism—one literally receives impressions: the passing trees overhead, the sun, the glint of sunlight on the ax. Again, during the rape scene, the camera seeks the sky, the sun, the trees, contrasting this with the two, wife and bandit. When the rape is consummated and just before we return to the prison courtyard for the conclusion of the bandit's story, the sun comes out from behind a branch, dazzling, shining directly into the lenses: a metaphor. Just as much a metaphor certainly as the scene shortly before where she drops her dagger and it falls point first to land upright, quivering in the ground; or the celebrated scene where Mifune is asleep and the two pass. He has mentioned the breeze in his testimony. Now we see it (accompanied by the cooling celesta on the sound track) as it ruffles his hair. He opens his eyes and sees it raising her veil. It is an extended metaphor, like a two-line poem. In Kurosawa's later films, this impressionism is not often seen, although there is a fine example at the end of *Sanjuro* where, after all the camellias have been sent off down the stream, there is a pause and then, as the bad man falls, a single blossom falls, all by itself, and is carried away—the perfect classic metaphor for the cut-short life.

Kurosawa in this film, and more than in any other, makes use of contrasting shots. A shot of the woman is held for a certain length of time. This is matched by a shot of the bandit, held for the same time. He intercuts these, back and forth, matching the timing so delicately that one does not notice the number of repeats while watching the film—and is surprised upon reading the script to discover that there are so many.

In the same way, he uses single close-ups to emphasize the triangular nature of the story. A shot of the woman is followed by a shot of the bandit is followed by a shot of the husband, and this process continues, going round and round as it were. Mostly, however, he insists upon the triangle through composition. The picture is filled with masterful triangular compositions, often one following directly after another, the frame filled with woman, bandit, husband, but always in different compositional relationships to each other. When the Japanese critics mentioned Kurosawa's "silent-film technique" they meant his great reliance upon composition—which with this film became, and still remains, one of the strongest elements of his film style.

Kurosawa's use of cinematic punctuation is always imaginative and, as we have seen, he is one of the few directors remaining who can intelligently use that most maligned of punctuation marks: the wipe. There is a fine use of it when the woman is waiting, during the bandit's story, and it (as always with Kurosawa) gives the effect of time, usually a short period of time, having elapsed. Here, as in *Ikiru*, the wipe is masterfully used. In *The Idiot*, on the other hand, Kurosawa was so unsure (because he was filming his favorite novel, by his favorite author, and doing it mainly for a then-uncooperative company) that he uses the wipe within a single scene, not once but many times, and the time indicated as having passed can only be a matter of seconds. An experiment, it remains in *The Idiot* entirely uncontrolled and very mannered—something which cannot be said of its use in *Rashomon*.

Kurosawa does not usually use fades (either in or out), tending to be suspicious of the softening effect they produce. Certainly the ending of *The Lower Depths*—it ends on an unexpected cut— would be far less effective with a fade-out. He uses it only, as in the opening and closing of *The Throne of Blood*, when he deliberately wants the effect of distance and uninvolvement. For Kurosawa the fade usually means the elegiac.

The dissolve, on the other hand, usually means time passing. The end of *Rashomon* is a beautiful example of this. The three men are standing under the gate and there is a series of dissolves moving closer and closer. This is almost a rhetorical device, since, in actuality, not much time could have passed. It is a formal gesture, a gesture which makes us look, and makes us feel. If the purpose is merely to indicate passage of time, however, Kurosawa has even simpler ways of doing it—one of the most imaginative in this picture is where the husband is waiting and his voice tells us that he waited a very long time. Here the effect is given through three long held shots with no dissolves or wipes at all—simply a long shot, followed by a far shot, followed by a medium close-up. These are used so consummately that one does not question that hours have passed.

Kurosawa's preoccupation with time (*the* preoccupation for any serious director) began with *Rashomon*. There are two kinds of time which concern him—and any other director. One is ostensible time —the time the story takes. The other is a certain kind of psychological time, the time that each sequence, and that each shot within this sequence, takes. The first kind is the kind which is appreciable to the audience as well. *Rashomon* is a series of flashbacks, all of them both true and false; *Ikiru,* on the other hand, is a film in which flashback leads into further flashback—the scene where the father finds the baseball bat, remembers the ballgame, remembers the operation, remembers the hospital, remembers the son going off to war. The second half of *Ikiru* is a series of flashbacks, in the *Citizen Kane* manner (a film which Kurosawa had not yet seen), which reconstructs the hero's life. The second kind of time is the kind of which no audience is aware—this is created in the alchemy of the cutting room, and it is telling that Kurosawa takes almost as long to cut as he does to shoot a film.

In *Rashomon* one remembers a series of seemingly actual, or at least realistic, actions. And yet the film—extraordinarily so, even for Kurosawa—is a mosaic. The average of the shorter cuts is 2 feet (1 1/3 seconds) and, although there are several shorter cuts, and although scenes also last for minutes (the dialogue scenes under the gate), still, the average length of each shot is shorter in *Rashomon* than in any other of Kurosawa's films. This always has the effect of reality on the screen. As Naoki Noborikawa has noticed, "In *Rasho-*

*mon* there is a scene where Tajomaru takes Takehiro [the husband] into the woods, then runs back and tells the woman that her husband has been bitten by a snake. The scenery through which the two together run to where he has left the husband tied up is full of great natural beauty, but the camera passes by it in one flash. I had thought that is was one shot, a swiftly moving pan. Seeing the film for the second time, however, I noticed that this was not so, and when I counted, on seeing it for the third time, I was surprised to discover that there were seven cuts in this small scene." As Kurosawa knew full well, one cuts fast and often for fast sections, slow and seldom for slow. But another reason for the extreme brevity of the *Rashomon* shots might be that the director knew he was asking this audience to look at the same material four or more times. He could not rely upon the novelty of the pictorial image to help sustain interest.

In addition, and maybe for the same reasons, he probably never moved the camera more than in *Rashomon*. The shooting script is full of directions to pan, to dolly in and out, etc. He used a favorite device of a dolly shot directly attached to a pan shot to get a continuity of action, and he was unusually careful of action continuity. This great mobility never calls attention to itself but gives the effect of continuous movement which we remember as being part of the style of the film.

All of these shots, stationary or moving, are superbly calculated as to their time on the screen and their effect there. There are few other directors who know so precisely the proper length for a given section of film. The shot of the dog carrying the human hand at the opening of *Yojimbo* is an example. One second less and we would not have known what he was carrying; one second more and the scene would have been forced, vulgar. In *Rashomon* the dagger drops into the ground and is allowed to quiver not often but just twice. All of the images are handled in this imaginative and economical manner. Kurosawa rarely makes a mistake in his timing, and the inner or psychological timing of *Rashomon* is perfection. There are 408 separate shots in the body of the film (with 12 more for titles, making a total of 420). This is more than twice the number in the usual film, and yet these shots never call attention to themselves—rather, they make it possible for us to feel this film, to be reached with immediacy, to be drawn into it, intellectually curious and emotionally aware. In a very special way, *Rashomon*—like any truly fine film—creates within its audience the very demand which it satisfies.

For a director as young as Kurosawa—he was then 40—and particularly for so young a Japanese director, the film is remarkably free from influences. Although some scenes owe much to Dovshenko's *Aerograd*, they owe nothing at all to Fritz Lang's *Siegfried* (an ostensible "influence" often mentioned), because the director has never seen it. The structure may owe something to *The Marriage Circle*, that Lubitsch film which Kurosawa—like most Japanese directors—remembers with affection and admiration, but the debt is very slight.

Of the style, Kurosawa has said only, "I like silent pictures and I always have. They are often so much more beautiful than sound pictures are. Perhaps they had to be. At any rate, I wanted to restore some of this beauty. I thought of it, I remember, in this way: One of the techniques of modern art is simplification, and I must therefore simplify this film." Simplification is also one of the techniques of Japanese art and long has been. Those who noticed a "Japanese" look about some of the scenes (mainly their composition, aside from temple architecture, sand gardens, and the like) were right, although the director had perhaps reached this through his own knowledge of simplified painting techniques in the West—those of Klee and Matisse, for example. Otherwise there is little "Japanese" influence. In fact, the film is the complete opposite of the ordinary Japanese historical film in that it questions, while they reaffirm; it is completely realistic, while they are always romantic; it is using its period as a pretext and a decoration, while the ordinary period film aims at simple reconstruction. Despite foreign commentators on the subject, there is absolutely no influence at all from classical Japanese drama. Only the sword-fighting techniques owe something to the modern Japanese stage. Anyone who has ever seen *Kabuki* will realize the enormous difference between its acting style and that of *Rashomon*. The acting in the film is naturalistic, in the Japanese sense of the word. It is apparently unrestrained, and it is in the

1. Toshiro Mifune as Tajomaru, the bandit.

2. Masayuki Mori as Takehiro, the samurai.

3. Machiko Kyo as Masago, wife of the samurai.

4. Masayuki Mori and Machiko Kyo.

5. Toshiro Mifune and Daisuke Kato, the police agent.

6. Masayuki Mori and Toshiro Mifune.

7. Toshiro Mifune and Machiko Kyo.

8. Minoru Chiaki as the priest, Kichijiro Ueda as the commoner, and Takashi Shimura as the woodcutter.

9. Machiko Kyo and Toshiro Mifune.

10. Toshiro Mifune and Masayuki Mori.

11. Toshiro Mifune and Machiko Kyo.

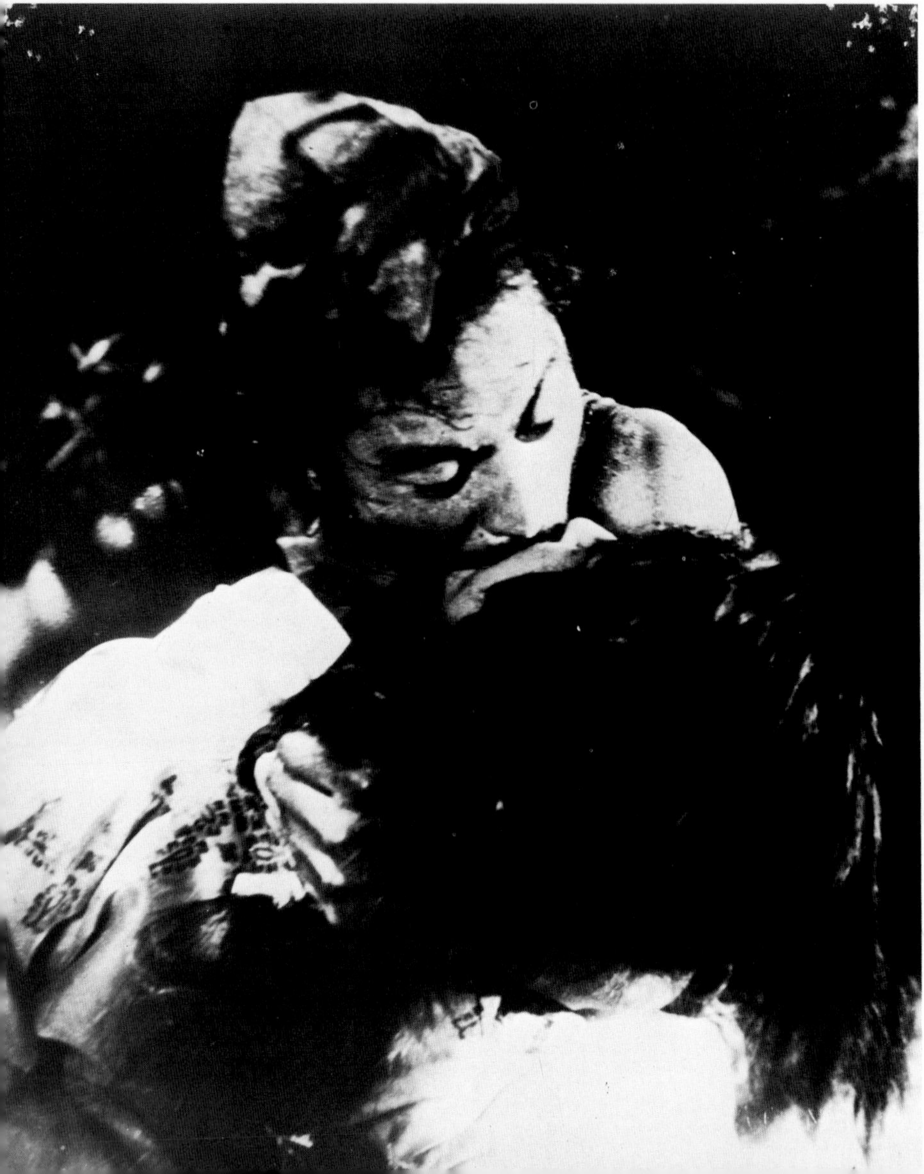

grand manner which the West once knew but has now almost lost. Indeed, Mifune as the bandit was so "grand" that even Japanese critics complained of overacting. There is another debt to the stage, however, although the stage is Japanese modern theater—the Shingeki. Since the budget was small, the sets (there are only two —both studio sets—the gate and the prison courtyard) are deliberately stylized, deliberately simplified in the manner of modern stage scenery (again, not *Kabuki* scenery, which is flamboyant, detailed, and very nineteenth century to the eye). Likewise, the costumes owe much to modern stage costumes, with their simplicity, their lack of ornament. Too—the music owes much to incidental-music methods on the modern Japanese stage.

That the music owes even more to another source is so notorious, some critics (Western) have admitted that the film was partially spoiled for them. This is not the fault of the composer. The late Fumio Hayasaka was one of Japan's most individual and creative composers, and it was Kurosawa himself who said, "Write something like Ravel's *Boléro*"—a work which in Japan had not yet become as clichéd as in the West. The composer complied and the results, as a matter of fact, do detract—particularly from the opening scenes.

Again and again in the films of Kurosawa one notices his musical tastes. Like most liberally educated Japanese, he has tended to like the chestnuts. He has already written how he once composed a thrilling scenario about cossacks while under the influence of *The Light Cavalry Overture*. Likewise one has noticed the strains of *Clair de lune* in *Drunken Angel* and an orgy of Schubert in *One Wonderful Sunday*. This continues, although as a music lover he has grown considerably more sophisticated and has recently spoken of his liking for Haydn, much in evidence in *Redbeard*, as is his new liking for late Brahms. Still, if one listens to the *Yojimbo* and *Sanjuro* scores, one finds not only the *Boléro* again (this time on the English horn), but also that the big *Sanjuro* theme bears more than a close family resemblance to the opening melody of the Liszt *Second Hungarian Rhapsody*.

The shooting time for the film was unusually short (it was completed within a matter of weeks, because most of the preproduction

work had been done for some time), and it is one of the few Kurosawa pictures that did not go over its budget. Daiei, although loudly
announcing that it had no idea what the picture was about, nevertheless exhibited it with some care. It was given a formal premiere
in what was then one of Tokyo's best theaters; the press was invited;
and it was given an initial run of two weeks (even now the usual
run is only a single week) at all the theaters in the Daiei chain. Contrary to later legend, it was not a box-office failure—it ranked fourth
in 1950's Daiei listings of best money-earners. Nor did the audience
seem to have trouble understanding it—although occasionally an
apprehensive theater manager would hire a *benshi,* a lecturer-
commentator, to talk throughout the film, giving hints as to what
it was about.

Daiei, although more pleased than not with its second Kurosawa
picture, made no attempt to detain him when he returned to Toho,
and after the second and third runs were completed, shelved the
picture. There it would probably have remained to this day had it
not been for a series of fortuitous circumstances which led to its
becoming the best-known Japanese film ever made.

Venice sent an invitation to Japan asking that a film be entered
in the film festival. This was before Japan became as well acquainted with film festivals as it is now, and there was consterna-
tion as to what to send. *Rashomon* was not even considered. In the
meantime, at the request of Venice, Guilliana Stramigioli, then
head of Italiafilm in Japan, had viewed a number of Japanese films,
had seen *Rashomon,* and had liked it. When she recommended it,
however, the suggestion was met with much opposition—particularly from Daiei, which had neither hope nor faith in the film. It
was with the greatest reluctance that they agreed to sending the
film to the 1951 Venice Festival, where it won first prize.

Its winning what was then the best-thought-of cinema prize came
as a profound shock to Japan. For one thing, it had not been made
for export and there remains a long-standing Japanese prejudice
that things not especially constructed for foreigners will not be
understood by them. For another, the Japanese critics had not liked
the film. Tadashi Iijima thought the film failed because of "its in-
sufficient plan for visualizing the style of the original stories"; Tat-

sushiko Shigeno objected to the language, saying that no robber would ever use words that big. Other critics thought the script was too complicated, or that the direction was too monotonous, or that there was too much cursing. What perhaps most surprised the Japanese, however, was that a historical film (and they continued to think of *Rashomon* as "historical" in the "costume-picture" sense of the word) should prove acceptable to the West. This eventually led to a rash of Western-aimed "historical" films—of which *Gate of Hell* is the only surviving example—but initially critics were at a loss to explain its winning the Venice prize and its consequent popularity in most other countries. Eventually, they decided that it was because *Rashomon* was "exotic" (in the sense that *Gate of Hell* is truly exotic—and little else) and that foreigners like exoticism. Even now it is the rare critic who will admit that *Rashomon* could have had any other appeal to the West.

Once the rare critic is found, however, he will say—as several have—that the reason the West liked it was because the reasoning in the picture was "Western," by which is meant analytic, logical, and speculative—processes which are indeed not often found in patterns of Japanese thought. Recognizing that the film questions reality yet champions hope, the critic says that this is not the Japanese way, and in a sense, he is right. Actually, of course, what had happened is that in this film (although not for the first time in Japanese cinema history), the confines of "Japanese" thought could not contain the director who thereby joined the world at large. *Rashomon* speaks to everyone, not just to the Japanese.

Kurosawa has said, "Japanese are terribly critical of Japanese films, so it is not too surprising that a foreigner should have been responsible for my film's being sent to Venice. It was the same way with Japanese woodcuts—it was the foreigners who first appreciated them. We Japanese think too little of our own things. Actually, *Rashomon* wasn't all that good, I don't think. Yet when people have said to me that its reception was just a stroke of luck, a fluke, I have answered by saying that they only say these things because the film is, after all, Japanese, and then I wonder: Why do we all think so little of our own things? Why don't we stand up for our films? What are we so afraid of?"

Though Daiei did not retain the director, it followed the usual maxim of film companies: If you have a success, repeat it. In the following year, Daiei's Keigo Kimura made *The Beauty and the Bandits,* which was taken directly from *Rashomon,* and the much better *Tale of Genji* by Kimisaburo Yoshimura. Kurosawa himself, his reputation enormously enhanced by the international success of the film, went back to Toho to make *Ikiru.* Show biz decided that Japan had made an unexampled breakthrough into the "foreign market," and the man on the street was as delighted over the Venice prize as he would have been had a Japanese athlete won an Olympics medal. Thus, in a way, the worth of *Rashomon* was partially obscured by its own success. It is only now, fifteen years later, that one realizes it is one of the few living films from Japan's cinematic past. Its frequent revivals in Japan, its frequent reshowings in other countries, its constant appearance in retrospectives, the fact that it is still talked about, still discussed, makes one finally realize that, along with *Ikiru* and *Seven Samurai,* it is a masterpiece.

# RASHOMON
## by TADAO SATO

In 1950 Akira Kurosawa made two films, *Scandal* and *Rashomon*. The former is a skillfully made small picture which lacks both the thematic strength and the formal beauty of Kurosawa's best work. *Rashomon* is, of course, the picture which made the Japanese art of cinema known in the West after it had won the Grand Prix at the Venice Festival the following year. More than this, however, the film is among the masterpieces of postwar Japanese cinema. One wants to believe that the West understood this, that its mere exoticism did not win the film the prize. And Alain Robbe-Grillet's remark that *L'Année dernière à Marienbad* was inspired by *Rashomon* would seem to indicate this until one considers the manifold differences between Kurosawa and Robbe-Grillet himself. In Japan the film was admired for its brilliance, and the critics put it among the year's ten-best films, but the general opinion was not inclined to call the film a masterpiece.

Akira Iwasaki has summed up the matter well when he says that "though the disbelief, indeed despair at human nature, the suspicion of objective truth and its reliability, did not win much sympathy from the masses of Japan, it was natural that these thoughts should appeal to West Europe, confronted as it was with a series of real crises." [1]

*From* The World of Akira Kurosawa (Kurosawa Akira no Sekkai) *by Tadao Sato. (Tokyo: Sanichishobo, 1968). Translated by Goro Sato. Edited by Donald Richie. Reprinted by permission of the author.*

[1] Akira Iwasaki, *A History of the Cinema.*

Yet one wonders if Rashomon indeed represents a disbelief and despair at human nature, a suspicion of objective truth and its reliability. It is difficult to believe that Kurosawa, who has shown the triumph of humanism in such films as *The Quiet Duel, Stray Dog,* and *Scandal,* should suddenly maintain a diametrically opposed opinion—he is simply not the kind of man interested enough in logic to play with its paradoxes. His intentions can be read into what he himself has said of the film. In the final sequence of *Rashomon,* there is the episode where the poor woodcutter takes care of the abandoned baby, resulting in the feeling that, despite what went before, human beings are naturally good. This episode has consequently been much criticized, been called unnatural and sentimental. Kurosawa himself defended it in an interview with Chiyota Shimizu.[2]

*Shimizu:* I think that episode with the baby is wrong—it sounds like a lesson in Christian charity.

*Kurosawa:* I have a word to say in its excuse. The spirit of our times is suspicious, and I am glad I have no part of it. I simply want people to be happy—though perhaps you may find a kind of escapism in my attitude.

*Shimizu:* I understand what you mean, but it seems to me that in the film it is all too sudden.

*Kurosawa:* It's strange—when people talk in a cynical manner, then everyone expresses approval; when someone speaks in an optimistic manner, however, the criticism is general. I question an attitude like that. However, maybe it is, as you say, all too sudden. Maybe I forced this ending on the film—but, on the other hand, I had no other way of ending it.

By which we understand that Kurosawa himself is far from being cynical.

*Rashomon* is based on the 1921 short story of Ryunosuke Akutagawa, "In a Grove," which in turn was based upon episodes in the tenth-century narrative, *Stories of the Past and Present (Konjaku Monogatari).* The original narrative is simple. A samurai traveling with his wife is tricked by a bandit who takes them to a grove, ties him up, and rapes the woman. After that the bandit goes away, the warrior and his wife continue their journey, although she blames him for not having prevented this occurrence. Akutagawa made this anecdote into a more complicated story by casting, in the form of seven confessions by the people who were implicated in the rape and murder.

A samurai named Takehiro is said to have been killed by a bandit named Tajomaru; the wife, named Masago, is supposed to have run off. At the police court Tajomaru speaks, as does Masago, and Takehiro himself, through a medium. They and the minor characters all testify and the three principals tell the story from their various viewpoints.

According to Tajomaru, he wanted to leave after raping Masago, but she clung to him, weeping, and saying that either he or her husband had to die. The bandit is proud to state that the won the duel.

According to Masago, after being raped by the bandit, she saw how her husband despised her for what had happened. He told her to kill herself and she, in her distraction, stabbed him.

According to Takehiro—through the medium—Tajomaru, after raping the wife, offered to marry her. She, wanting to go off with him, asked him to kill her husband. Surprised at this, he left her then and there. Therefore he, the husband, killed himself. This is as far as Akutagawa goes.

The story was adapted by Shinobu Hashimoto, a then-unknown writer who had worked with the late Mansaku Itami. Another director, Kiyoshi Saeki, who had also been affiliated with Itami, showed the scenario to Kurosawa and introduced the young writer. From the first, Kurosawa was interested in the work but decided, with Hashimoto's help, to add a fourth confession not in the original—that of a woodcutter. Here the story was that Tajomaru decided to marry Masago and challenged Takehiro to a duel. He, however, protested that such a woman was not worth fighting over. Masago, however, goaded them into a duel, during which she fled.

The episode of the woodcutter sounds as though he is lying, particularly when it comes out that he must himself have stolen the missing murder weapon, the dagger. Yet except for this single point, there was no reason for his lying. After all, the episode of the wood-cutter was added not to complicate but to point out that each of the more interested parties had his own reasons for telling the story the way he did—to show himself to be honest.

Actually, *Rashomon* is a work that states a strong belief in the worth of human beings, as well as an equally strong belief in objective truth. Otherwise, there would have been no significance in adding the woodcutter's confession. Although the woodcutter may lie, we are not therefore to draw the conclusion that truth is incomprehensible. Rather, his story shows the humanity of the other three, just as his rescuing the baby at the end shows his own.

Actually, talk about whether *Rashomon* is humanistic or not is a bit beside the point. If Kurosawa had wanted to prove a humanistic thesis, he probably would not have chosen this material. If he had wanted to prove an antihumanistic thesis he would undoubtedly not have ended the picture as he did. One of the things we know about his intentions is that he was from the first interested in the most cinematic way to tell a story. That he did not think of his film as containing any philosophic or spiritual message is shown by his words upon receiving the Venice prize, when he said that he would have been more gratified if the prize had been given to a film with more contemporary meaning.

*Rashomon* is a masterpiece because of the way it is made, because of the director's interpretation, his style, his technique. Just how brilliant it is we discover if we compare it to Martin Ritt's *The Outrage,* which is an adapation of the same scenario and turned out to be so commonplace as not worth the viewing.

One remembers brilliant scenes in the Kurosawa film: the wood-cutter (Takashi Shimura) in the grove, the sun shining through the leaves; the wife (Machiko Kyo) assaulted by the bandit (Toshiro Mifune) while her husband (Masayuki Mori) is tied to a tree; when he forcibly kisses her, the sun shines into her eyes, dazzling her. This last is interesting enough to be examined in detail:

> 161 Long shot. The woman in the foreground, sobbing; Tajo-maru in the background. He stalks up to her, she lunges yet again, but now he grabs and holds her. (15 seconds)

162 Close-up of the husband watching them; he bows his head. (5 seconds)

163 Close-up. The woman claws Tajomaru's face; he wrests her head free and pushes her to the ground (camera tilts down); she struggles but he kisses her. (7 seconds)

164 The sky (pan) seen through the branches of the trees. (2 seconds)

165 Close-up of the bandit kissing her; she stares straight up. (4 seconds)

166 The sky (pan) seen through overhead branches. (2 seconds)

167 Close-up from reverse angle; Tajomaru holding her, kissing her. (1 second)

168 The sky and trees. The camera no longer pans; the sun shining brilliantly through the branches. (3 seconds)

169 Large close-up from reverse angle: Tajomaru kissing the woman as she stares blankly at the sun. (3 seconds)

170 The sun through the branches; slowly the scene goes out of focus. (4 seconds)

171 Large close-up. The woman closes her eyes. (4 seconds)

172 Large close-up of the dagger in her hand, Tajomaru tightly gripping her wrist. Her fingers loosen, the dagger drops to the ground. (3 seconds)

173 Large close-up of the dagger sticking point first in the ground. (2 seconds)

174 Middle shot of Tajomaru's back, the woman in his arms. The camera slowly dollies toward them. Her hand encircles his back, her fingers move caressingly; she tightens her grip on him: she is giving herself. (11 seconds)[3]

All of this action—and it is merely a bandit kissing a woman—is edited rhythmically, and divided into fourteen different shots, into which are accented over and over again the close-ups of the sun. She is herself lost in the dazzle of this sun and the camera moves forward to see the beads of sweat on the bandit's back, glittering under this same sun, as beautiful as diamonds, and in her caressing of this sweat her ecstasy is suggested.

[3] In the original Japanese edition, this section of the script was taken from *An Anthology of Famous Scenarios, Kinema-Jumpo-Sha,* October 1952. In this edition the passage is rendered as it appears in Robert Hughes and Donald Richie, eds., *Rashomon* (New York: Grove Press, Inc., 1969).

What is lacking in Ritt's *The Outrage* is precisely this exultation, this ecstasy face to face with the sun, this psalm to naked humanity, which gazes at the sun with eyes wide open and feels no regret at exposing itself freely under this sunlight. Extraordinary as this passage is, it does not illustrate the theme of the film. It is followed at once by Takehiro's confession, in which such exultation is made to appear as though it is a crime.

*Rashomon* is filled with such marvellous images, which once seen are not to be forgotten. There is the sequence where Tajomaru, having tied up Takehiro, runs back shouting to get Masago, the light of the sun dazzling among the leaves; there is in this extremely rhythmically edited sequence—fourteen short shots in all—one of the most brilliant examples of fluent beauty in Japanese cinema.

Here I might mention that I feel that, historically, this kind of passage in Japanese period films is always used in the same kind of situation: in showing us the pathetic beauty of the pursued. This kind of passage has been created by an awareness of the sufferings of someone trying to get away. In these scenes, where the assailant springs upon the prey, Kurosawa is within a known genre but has illuminated it with crystalline beauty. One might indeed find in this passage the meaning of the film. Continuously there are cuts back to the great gate, Rashomon itself, with a heavy rain pouring as though it is trying to wash away the greatest of sins.

And then we must ask the question, What is it then in these desires and exultations that requires mobilization of such sun, such rain? To commit a crime and then to face it, to reach ecstasy itself, looking straight into the sun—such an image has perhaps never before been seen in Japanese cinema. Sin, evil, these belong to the dark night, the melancholy mood—or used to, at any rate. The so-called *taiyo-zoku* (rebellious younger generation) pictures, that came into vogue four years after *Rashomon,* often enough showed the ecstasy of sin under a midsummer sun, yet few of such films in any way paralleled *Rashomon,* except for Kon Ichikawa's 1956 picture, *Punishment Room (Shokei no Heya).* What they mostly lacked, despite their casual acceptance of daytime sin, were such things as a continual contrasting downpour, almost washing away the devastated streets of Kyoto, as if to deny an overflowing consciousness of crime.

Here Kurosawa crystallized a genuine style, one that had little to do with faith or lack of it in human beings, but much to do with the exultations and atonements of the individual. The director often uses fierce winds, violent rains, or sunlight enough to give sunstroke. Such are apparently just exaggerated gestures to ensure the effect of dramatic complications, and so they are in his minor works. They are, however, more. Violent wind, rain, light, all have the function of separating a character from his social functions, of confronting him with his own inner reactions. They reflect inner desires or fears, they have nothing to do with a moral consciousness, which is, in itself, social. Not to feel hunted or driven, but to admit desire and self-confidence; not to blame their sins on others but to confess it serenely in the face of the sun and the rain—this is the true pursuit of the genuine self, and it is this that has been so largely lacking in Japanese cinema and could have appeared only now when the moral authority of society was weakened.

Machiko Kyo's most impressive scene is the episode of Masago's confession, in which, after having been violated, she goes to her husband, then sees the scorn in his eyes, and cries, "Don't, don't look at me like that!" She paces back and forth in front of him, near hysteria. The acting of both was most impressive, their best performances in anything. And here, Kurosawa—in a sequence comprising about twenty cuts—cuts back and forth carefully between the characters, who both writhe in separate ways under the feeling of shame, gazing into each other's eyes but each fearing the gaze of the other. These cuts are so adjusted—dollies backward and forward, pans left and right—that the result is a vivid picturization of shame, as though the camera itself were in agony.

Yet the woman, placed in the situation of utmost shame, instead of being conquered by this emotion, finally and boldly stares, putting her full emotional power into this gaze; and the man is stabbed to death and yet continues his gaze of cold contempt—in short, all shameful feelings we see turned into a psalm of life, this clashing together has penetrated and destroyed the emotion of shame by transcending it.

Each of these shots is very short, and their succession gives us the feeling that we are moving along with the camera. She does not want to look at him, yet she must; he, likewise, cannot keep his eyes from her. These shots of them draw their gazes as though a cord existed between the two of them, and us.

Seen in the context of the story, this sequence seems to be portraying only the egoism of the man, the grief of the woman—yet, owing to the acting, to the camera work of Kazuo Miyagawa, the direction of Kurosawa, something far more important results: Only a consciousness of shame can restore beauty to the individual who has lost it. To be conscious of shame is the same as self-respect. For Kurosawa, this point is, I think, the emotional basis for his moral.

# RASHOMON
## by NINO GHELLI

The Japanese cinema cannot boast of an important tradition; its works (with the exception of *Earth* of Tomu Uchida) have not until today aroused any interest beyond that of a simple curiosity concerning its use—almost always primitive and naive—of the medium.

Compared to preceding Japanese films, *Rashomon,* with its extreme technical perfection and its consummate stylistic refinement, must be considered an important exception. As far as style is concerned, it shows a maturity and expressiveness which are every bit the equal of the works of the most sophisticated European authors, proving yet once again the absurity of a critical philosophy based on one set of cultural values. In ascertaining the aesthetic validity of a work, we are not in the least interested in the level of technical and stylistic evolution of which the author has given evidence in his use of his chosen expressive means, but rather how fully he has expressed his own poetic world, which, since it sums up the whole personality of the artist, also determines how he will use the technical means at his disposal. Despite the sterile attempts of certain pseudohistorians or pseudocritics, convinced that a work of film must be considered as something inferior to works expressed in other media because of the supposed distance between lyrical inspiration and the technical means used to convey it, it should by now be only too clear that it is not the stylistic means used or the particular technical complexity of the actual filming of the work that render it less of an art

*From* Bianco e Nero *13, no. 3 (March 1952). Reprinted by permission of the publisher. Translated by Robert M. Connolly.*

than the other arts. Arnheim has already taught us that when judging a film aesthetically, we should look at the live film on the screen, completely forgetting about everything from the original inspiration to the technical particulars, everything that took place in the preparatory phase of the film, which is born only at the moment of its projection on the screen as a completed work. But, naturally, a similar conclusion, which would seem elementary and logical even to a mediocre philosopher, is rejected by all those improvised "masters" of literary or musical criticism or of the figurative arts who infest our poor cinema, while at the same time showing a profound disdain for it, affirming continuously that the cinema, after only fifty years of life, cannot claim that its works have the same validity as a painting, a novel, etc. All of which, even if it could be proved historically, would change absolutely nothing in an *a priori* theory such as aesthetics.

Similar grotesque absurdities are encouraged by the incoherencies of all those who, in order to sustain the artistic validity of a film, decide that it lies either in its content (although it is lacking in expressive significance), be it sociological, moralistic, or political, or in a sterile and Byzantine formalism, lost in a narcissistic love for arabesques. Whereas it should be all too obvious that a work of art can be born only of a perfect synthesis of imagination and feeling in the creative process, which is objectivized immediately through the technical means.

Thus, apropos of *Rashomon*, a film, as we have said, of unquestioned intelligence and notable stylistic brilliance, there are those who have acclaimed it as something miraculous, as a perfect work of art, and even as an example of a new film grammar. Furthermore— and it doesn't happen very often—it has been showered with praise by the "content" partisans, evidently seduced by the ideological affirmations and the philosophical problems on human nature which the film sets forth, and by the formalists, captivated by its exquisite figurative composition, by its plastic values, by its skillful photography and lighting. *Rashomon* is undoubtedly a significant work, for the richness of the problems confronted, and for the attempt, ofttimes successful, to confer added meaning to the image through heightening its plastic and figurative elements. Its virtues are many;

they cannot, however, redeem in full its defects and assure it a place in the immortal realm of art.

A strong contrast is in fact clearly apparent between the substantially naive and elementary poetic world of Kurosawa, obvious in the narrative construction and the theme of the story, and the refined, almost decadent, use of stylistic devices, producing an inevitable lack of sincerity, or if one prefers, of coherence, which can only invalidate the work on a purely aesthetic level, even though it may retain its importance on a historical and cultural level.

The author's singular naiveté is clearly evident in the way in which he begins with a thematic construction dear to his Oriental spirit because of its obvious moralistic intent, and then tries to clothe it in a structural and narrative complexity clearly foreign to that world, thus producing an inevitable element of discord. The result is a disconcerting contrast between the fablelike construction of the story itself (with everything laid out in geometrical symmetry, in which each story ends up at the scene where it began, along with digressions of moralistic commentary, and at the end a rhetorical and forced conclusion is tacked on in order to resolve the work with a thematic statement which is extraneous to the characters and the story), and the unfolding of the narrative in episodes which are outwardly complex, because of the uncertain character of the narrative solutions, and for the problematic nature of the characters; without, however, this narrative complexity, which should go to the roots of the most fundamental problems of man's interior life—those of truth and guilt—ever assuming an authentic dramatic character in an inevitable conflict resulting in a poetic statement of the author's point of view.

This gives rise to a feeling of useless persistence from the outside on the part of Kurosawa on a subject which should instead have been constructed from the inside, especially with regard to the characters. These characters, some of whose façades have been exaggerated, especially the bandit, while others are too conventional and others too symbolic, are disconcerting and unconvincing in their one-dimensionalness. They have been drawn in too simple a way to make acceptable the psychological complexity which the author meant them to have, and which would justify their actions and make them dramatically believable. So that in effect the problematic nature of the characters and the complex entanglements of their adventure, which becomes even murkier and more contradictory in the versions of the three figures who experienced it, does not find a poetic justification to back up the general statement made in the fourth tale, that each person, when reliving his own experiences, tends fatally to invest them with a heroic significance, in which he himself stands out and is shown in the most favorable light. Not, therefore, a statement of a universal impossibility of true communication among men, because in each of us there lies a subjective reality which is unfathomable and different from every other one, and therefore of the nonexistence of an objective reality, a thesis which he seems to want to affirm at the beginning of the film (hence certain critics' inexact linking of the film's meaning to a certain European school of narrative, and, in particular, theater, whose principal exponent was our Pirandello), but rather the simplest kind of statement on the essential and almost atavistic meanness of spirit existing in each of us, impregnating human life in its very essence, putting in doubt even the existence of God, if the perpetuity of existence itself and the sudden manifestations of Providence did not redeem men from their baseness. A thesis which obviously could have had a total poetic validity had the author imparted an emotional conviction to his characters and situations, which instead seem to have been conceived and developed with great intelligence and refinement of technique, but never presented or judged with a sincere humanity which would have invested them with universal meaning.

To prove this, one may point out the structural incongruities between the characters of the three central figures of the story and the little "chorus" made up of the woodcutter, the thief, and the priest; the need felt by the author to resort to those unfortunate, repetitious, moralistic commentaries to each tale; and the obvious rhetoric of the finale, which resolves the work simplistically and optimistically, proving conclusively that Kurosawa lacked a true critical vision of the world he was describing.

The intellectualism revealed in many narrative passages and in certain aspects of the psychological construction (cold and exterior as it is) of the characters is even more evident in the extreme refinement of the film's style. Always in evidence is a painter's unfailing sense of the plasticity of the image; his carefully wrought chiaroscuro effects, particularly in the lovely sequence of the walk in the forest of the samurai and his wife, in which the framing of the image, seen in long shot, the light streaming down from above, the warm tone of the photography, the actors' costumes, the leisurely cadence of the editing, together with the perfectly captured physical sensations, such as the silence of the spot, the calm of the hour, the heat of the afternoon, all go together to create a mood perfectly consonant with the spirit of the story.

This ability to utilize his sense of the image to convey dramatic meaning is evident throughout. One thinks, for example, of the placing of the characters in the shot, according to rigidly geometrical lines, not only evidencing a highly refined visual sense, but serving as well to illustrate the precise dramatic rapport among them, the most important characters being shown in close-up. In the sequences of the three tales in particular, the dramatic resources of the depth of field are combined with a skillful use of camera angles, composition, camera movement, and the relationship between the human material and the scenic, to emphasize the relationships among the characters; the shot of the woman huddled in a medium-long shot in the arch formed by the legs of the man in the foreground to indicate his domination over her; the succession of shots, with the rhythm steadily increasing, in which two of the three characters appear on different levels along the horizon, forming a triangle which closes them in, showing the insignificance of the men in front of the immensity of the temple, indicating their human fragility; and the shots of the court, in which the camera becomes the disembodied judge, representing the conscience, and generating a sense of anguish and mystery; the succession of beginning shots of the woodcutter's race through the woods, in which the shot becomes more and more close-up, and the cutting more rapid, perfectly rendering the breathless tension of the moment; the sequences of the duels, in which the prodigious mobility of the camera confers an extraordinarily dynamic feeling to the struggle; the sequence of the rape, in which the camera, revolving around the entwined figures, manages to suggest the woman's awakening sensuality.

No less meticulous is the author's use of the elements of scenery and sound: the stifling atmosphere of the woods, which sets the mood of the whole film; the surreal quality of the police court, summarily sketched and yet intensely effective, with its low wall, limiting the horizon and creating a closed-in, trapped feeling; the gigantice temple, representing the eternal survival of the divinity, in contrast to men frantically pursuing their petty ambitions. Sound plays an essential role throughout most of the film, from the roar of the storm and the pelting rain at the beginning, and the divine wrath (somewhat naively, as also at the end of the film, where the pale sun through the clouds represents a resurgence of hope), to the obsessive whistling of the wind in the tale of the sorceress, to the transference in her of the man's voice, with its striking effect; to the heavy breathing of the two duellers, a sign of their terror, in the fourth tale. And if the abovementioned formal virtues and tasteful and sophisticated use of stylistic devices do not quite manage to confer on the work that aesthetic unity without which there cannot be art, it is because of the fact that they, rather than springing from a genuine and instinctive expressive need of the author, are instead the result of careful and meticulous reflection. And it is because they have been carried out so deliberately and so cerebrally that these stylistic effects cannot be considered as true art, but rather as an aesthetic exercise and as decadence, albeit of the most refined sort. Kurosawa's prodigious skill in the use of camera movement, especially in the fourth tale, falls fatally into the realm of exhibitionism, of the desire to dazzle; just as the excellence of his sense of composition becomes annoyingly deliberate, in his penchant for arranging his characters in ways which are aesthetically striking, but too obviously studied and unspontaneous, so that they all end up in the category of formula, like the bandit, who (because of the excesses of the interpreter as well) seems conventional and exterior, or like the samurai, described in the most stereotyped manner, and devoid of any human quality, or like the woman, who is without a solid psychological character and thus lacking in aesthetic coherence.

This preoccupation with style, sometimes impassioned and functional, more often elaborate and unfeeling, is present also in the rhythm of the editing, brilliant, as we have said, in the tense scene where the woodcutter finds the body, of exceptional rhythmic impetus in the duelling scenes, and in the scene of the woman's tale; but at other times heavy, awkward, unconvincing. And though the infraction of the conventional rules of editing seems at times deliberate and carefully thought out, as in the splicing to build up the finale, that achieved by dissolves for the purpose of arriving at a slow and spacious rhythm; at other times errors of editing give the narrative a disconcerting sense of confusion and arbitrariness.

In conclusion, the film is full of truly excellent moments, in which heart-felt inspiration breathes life into richly poetic episodes, such as the scene of the woman's tale, in which the composition, the relationship among the characters, and the expert rhythm of the shots all combine to create a sort of dance of death; or the scene of the first duel, with its extraordinary narrative vigor. But alongside these moments are much less successful things in which the rhythm lags, and there are dead spots which cannot be redeemed by skillful technique alone, such as the scene of the woodcutter's tale, and the beginning and the end of the film, a vacuous prologue and epilogue having little relevance to the central story itself.

However, despite its air of decadence, the film possesses, as we have said, an undeniable nobility. If only at moments, and not too frequent ones, it rises to the level of true poetry, there is present at all times—and often to an admirable degree—a precise style.

# The Japanese Film: Inquiries
# and Inferences
## by VERNON YOUNG

It is no doubt unavoidable, our culture being what it is—an up-
start and afraid in a world it never made—that more nonsense than
pertinence has been uttered and written on the subject of the Japanese film. At this stage of our familiarity, the main obligations of
criticism should be to abjure responsibility for knowledge it can't be
expected to display and to try clearing the air by asking a few honest
questions. Most of us who write about films may as well relax and
confess that we know nothing at first hand about Japanese movie
production; that all we have as data has come to us from press sheets,
from quick consultation with the nearest Japanese bystander, or
from a handful of factual essays; that whatever else we may know of
Japanese art is the sum (probably meager) of having taken an "intelligent interest" in Japanese prints, of having been exposed aca-
demically to the matter of Japanese influence on the architecture of
Frank Lloyd Wright, of having read two Japanese novels and a few
slim volumes of poetry, of exploring, post-*Rashomon*, whatever we
have been able to find useful in the way of analogy and of seeing
the "unaccredited" performances of *Kabuki*. Beyond this, except for
the fortunate few who may have been in Europe with sufficient fre-
quency since 1951 to see others of the dozen or more Japanese films

*From* The Hudson Review *8, no. 3 (Autumn 1955). Copyright* ©
*1955 by The Hudson Review, Inc. Reprinted by permission of the pub-
lisher.*

exhibited there, we have been shown precisely five in the United States on which to establish generalities. (Of these, two—*The Impostor* and *Hiroshima*—scarcely merit extended consideration, and we owe the selection of the big three to the enterprise and good taste of Mr. Edward Harrison.) This little piggy stayed at home and he is by now somewhat wearied by those who primarily see the Japanese motion picture (let's just say *Rashomon, Ugetsu,* and *The Gate of Hell*) as a by-product of Japanese decorative and theater arts. He is equally wearied by the Orientalists (home-grown or otherwise) who are patently well informed on the minutiae of Japanese culture but who know little or nothing of cinematic art.

There is a prevalent and not altogether accurate analogy in emergent use between the Japanese film and Japanese "painting." Before this easy observation goes much further, we should plainly ask *what kind* of painting is implied for reference and which of the three films usually invoked actually exemplifies, in more than a superficial way, such a comparison. We have been specifically informed that Kazuo Miyagawa, the cinematographer of *Rashomon* and *Ugetsu,* is a student of traditional Japanese art, and we may assume that a large number of the technicians on these films share his absorption. By reference to single frames in *Ugetsu,* I would infer that both India-ink drawings and the woodblocks of Hiroshige might very likely have been Miyagawa's inspiration. But a specialist would have to confirm my inference and further specify the models, if any, for the photographic style of *Rashomon,* which, to my view, nowhere suggests Japanese painting in any media. And in *The Gate of Hell,* quite dissimilar effects are achieved by Kohei Sugiyama, owing as much to their composition in Eastman color and to their formal derivation from the constructs of Eisenstein (in the opening episodes, especially) as to their kinship with kakemonos, woodblock prints, or folding screens. I am now prepared to add to the confusion myself by contending that the film which to me egregiously suggests Japanese water-color-and-ink textures is not a Japanese film at all, but Arne Sucksdorf's occult documentary of Swedish wildlife, *The Great Adventure.*

Both the photography and music of the Japanese films have come in for a certain amount of cavil. Here the purist struts and frets his hour. I have heard an allegedly responsible teacher of aesthetics claim that the lighting in *Ugetsu* was "too dim." And in the magazine *Film Culture* (March–April 1955), an excessively disgruntled "Oriental critic" (he was so programmed), Ben Pinga by name, after donning a hair shirt, took to task the producers of *The Gate of Hell* for their failure to make the Buddhist message more explicit, for not being consistent in their musical scoring, and, above all, for having "played up the visual splendor of the subject at the expense of its ideas and meanings." Leaving to someone with more time on his hands that charming cognate, "ideas and meanings," I'll content myself with fearing that the accusation of which it is the nub will meet with scant agreement. Without conceding that generally held opinions are more valid than minority ones, I find Mr. Pinga's downright perverse, but I daresay that the degree of beauty one can support in a given context is not measurable. The more recherché quibbles fall strictly within the province of the experts, but I am not intimidated by Mr. Pinga's self-identification with this category, in the face of his innocent belief that the cameraman of *The Gate of Hell* was also the camerman of *Ugetsu*. Nor am I much more impressed by the scolding, every bit as stern, administered by Gordon Hendricks (same magazine, same issue) to the musical director of *The Gate of Hell*. In considerable detail and with an air of authority as indisputable as his petulance, Mr. Hendricks discoursed on the nature and social usages of the *Koto,* the *samisen,* and the *shakubyoshi,* and crushingly deplored the occasional employment of Western strings and of drums "played in a Western scale." I would be willing to knuckle under to Mr. Hendricks' agitated defense of authenticity and I'd even promise myself to listen more objectively when I see *The Gate of Hell* again, if it were not for the very grave impasse into which the writer led himself by his retrospective criticism of the *Rashomon* sound track.

Proudly involving Archer Winsten of the New York *Post* in his shock reaction, as if this agreement certified his sense of outrage, Mr. Henricks fulminated against Ravel's *Boléro* used "to back up a 13th-century legend" (a description which, while we're brushing the subject, requires qualification; the literary material on which Kurosawa based his adaptation came from two short stories by Ryunosuke

Akutagawa, who committed suicide in 1927). I think we must all have been alarmed by the *resemblance* of the bandit theme to the *Boléro* (that it is literally the *Boléro,* note for note, I doubt) but I hope a majority of the baffled suspended their judgment in favor of the belief that Kurosawa might reasonably be trusted, like any serious artist, to know exactly what he was doing. That Kurosawa did know is ably supported by James F. Davidson in a most edifying article, "Memory of Defeat in Japan: A Reappraisal of *Rashomon,*" [1] which is indispensable reading for any further speculation on Kurosawa's masterly film. To summarize a single point of Mr. Davidson's exposition: At one level of interpretation, the bandit represents—the West! From this clue, you may deduce the ramifications for yourself, but I urge you to read Mr. Davidson. In any case, you can see at once the sardonic function of the music's alleged impurity.

*Stylization* is probably the most ambiguous conception currently overexercised. A semantic difficulty, I'm sure. No one bothers to distinguish between the stylized, the conventional, the generic, the abstract, and the stereo-typical. Japanese milieu, in art and life, being what it is—rigorously fashioned with a consistency which in our world occurs only under special conditions of place, economy, temperament, and influence—our interpretation of its quality is pardonably confused. Sometimes pardonably. Into an aperitif served to the readers of *Fashion and Travel,* "Style: and the Japanese," Truman Capote stirred a doubtful ingredient: "A half-comparison might be made with Restoration comedy: there is at least the same appreciation of the artificial; *and it is true* that in the gangster thriller and cowboy genre Americans have produced *a classically stylized form* of code and behavior." (The italics are mine—believe me!) Mr. Moritoh, meet Little Caesar and Mr. Shane. I'm sure you three gentlemen will have much to discuss. . . . Mr. Capote is in safer hands when he repeats Arthur Waley's observation that a principal characteristic of the Japanese aesthetic is dread of the explicit. But I am certain that different levels of aesthetic and, conceivably, different occasions, are here involved. *The Gate of Hell* affords many instances

---

[1] *Antioch Review,* XIV-4 (December 1954). [See this volume, pp. 119-28.]

of this dread, expressed with lovely indirection, but it also features that extraordinary moment when the samurai spits a mouthful of water into the face of the unconscious Lady Kesa. Sexual insight has not often been rendered so ruthlessly, with no dread whatever of the explicit. And *Rashomon* is as fearlessly expounded, which brings me into argument with another authority.

Since Harold Strauss has the support of past residence in Japan, I have read with some attention and even humility his recent articles on the subject, but when he describes Machiko Kyo's laughter (in her taunting of husband and brigand in *Rashomon*) as stylized, I am prompted to challenge further what seems to me an increasingly general misuse of the term. Quite simply, stylization implies a *reduction* or a *crystallizing* of elements, but I appeal to Elie Faure's elaborate definition (evoked, incidentally, by this very matter of the Japanese principle, in Volume III of his *History of Art*) to assist the relevance of my objection.

> An erroneous distinction has often been made between the process of reason which consists in stylizing a form and the process of instinct which tends to idealize it. Idealization does not re-form an object; it reconstructs and completes it so as to deduce the most general, the purest, and the most hopeful meaning that the object has for man. Stylization adapts it to its decorative function by systematizing the characteristics which appear in practically a consistent manner when the form is studied. The artist saw that all forms and gestures and all architectures in repose or in movement retained certain dominant qualities which defined them in our memory and which, when accentuated by schematic processes, could be applied to decoration with the utmost exactitude. . . .

If this distinction is as acceptable to others as it is to me, the application of "stylized" to the scene designated can surely be called into question. To my feeling, that moment of laughter is the almost intolerable climax of a sequence characterized by primordial realism. Miss Kyo's laugh may well ring in one's ears after the last film has faded from the last screen as a consummate outcry of subhuman derision. . . . I would say that this actress's face makeup was conventionalized, if you like, as it was for *Ugetsu* and for *The Gate of Hell*, and that the court sequences of *Rashomon* (where the film audience is the tribunal), in passive face-front contrast to the restless movement of the camera in the woods, were formalized, after the suggestive mode of the *Noh* drama, as Mr. Strauss pointed out in his *Harper's* article.[2] The meticulous relationship of figures to the architectural spaces wherein they sit or move, a conspicuous feature of *The Gate of Hell*, but not uniquely Japanese, is simply a theatrical, or plastic, sense of proportion; it would illustrate Faure's sense of the stylized if its gestures and other elements were submitted to an elliptical and unrealistic continuity. (Yesterday's European Expressionist theatre was, in its own way, as stylized as *Noh*.) Only in *The Impostor,* among the films shown here, a commodity item of the Shochiku Corporation, owners of the *Kabuki-za,* is there considerable, if not subtle, treatment of this kind (the mock duels, the fixed character traits, and so forth).

The reception of Japanese film acting has not been unanimously charitable. Embarrassed by the vehemence of the Japanese actor, and even by his repose (notable in Kazuo Hasegawa—Moritoh in *The Gate of Hell*—who generates tremendous force while sitting completely still), many Westerners attempt to account for their discomfort at the phenomenon by some such explanation of it as stylized or "artificial" acting. When the performers, seized by paroxysms of violence or anguish, throw themselves on the ground, bellow, grunt, and gnash their teeth, embarrassment may give way to facetiousness. From unexpected areas of the critical world, where you would suppose some effort might be made to rise above a subjective reaction to alien manners, have come unwarranted disclaimers, of *Ugetsu* markedly. John McCarten's flippant review of this film in *The New Yorker* was the least excusable; I make this assertion not from any belief in the balefulness of wit (I usually find Mr. McCarten quite funny) but from an assumption that jeering at an unfamiliar mode is not a vice permissible to a critic. At least, not without more authority than I suspect Mr. McCarten can lay claim to. The most unflattering verdict on Japanese histrionics was delivered long since by

[2] "My Affair with Japanese Movies," July 1955.

the French poet, Henri Michaux, in his ferociously brilliant travel memoir, *A Barbarian in Asia,*[3] but it was the fruit not of a single film but of several months of theatergoing in the Orient.

> No actor in the world bawls like the Japanese with so little result. He does not speak his part, he mews it, belches it, and he trumpets, brays, neighs and gesticulates like one possessed, and in spite of it all I do not believe him.
>
> All this is done on the side, "to decorate." The frightful contortions he makes in the effort to represent his sufferings merely express the hell of a trouble he is taking to express suffering; it is suffering expressed by a man who no longer knows the meaning of it (a lot of esthetes, all of them) in front of an audience of esthetes, equally ignorant of the subject.
>
> A loud voice that reeks of prejudice a thousand miles away, of life taken up by the wrong end, a background of ancient impostures and obligations, and a series of second-rate notions, but spelled with a capital letter, in the midst of which like the voices of the Categorical Imperative (the great master of Japan) the poor characters move about, victims, subordinate creatures, but giving themselves, as one might expect, great swashbuckling airs, with a peculiarly decorative type of courage, and there is such a lack of variety that one sees why in the *No* plays they wear a mask and why at Osaka the actors are simply wooden marionettes, lifesize.

There is much more of this, very amusing, very perceptive, and very cruel. If I had less respect for Michaux's fabulous gift for psychological impressionism I would hesitate to present such a persuasive corroboration of the latent xenophobes among us. As it is, I am willing to accept his prejudice for the sake of his vivid accent, but I reserve the right to claim that I've not been similarly affected by actors in the Japanese film. Furthermore, I am strongly convinced that however "decorative" *Kabuki*-trained actors may have seemed to Michaux on the stage in the early 1930s, they have been forced by the exigencies of the interior drama which has constituted the screen-

---

[3] New York: New Directions, 1949. Tr. Sylvia Beach. First published in France, 1933.

plays to substantiate their emotions by a more complete involvement. Clearly the principals of the three films under discussion understand the meaning of the suffering *they* are expressing! And this, I think, is not the least wonderful result of the Daiei company's so-called compromise with the West. If the psychological realism and the dynamic editing of these films is a consequence of Western influence on Japanese style, we cannot but be gratified by their instinctive conquest of our domain. The motion picture is by its nature and its origin Western. A *pure* Japanese film is a contradiction in terms, for it could only be an even more awkward compromise between film and theatre than *The Impostor* has verified. The "stylized" theatre of Japan—*Kabuki* and *Noh,* if not *Bunraku*—will presumably survive in its own right, but the Japanese film will have to develop away from the broadest theatre conventions in order to be film at all, and a transformation of the acting technique is naturally of initial importance.

As a matter of related fact, many people find a full expression of emotion equally intolerable in our own theatre and movies. I have seen audiences highly disturbed by a passionately committed Shakespearean actor or one from the Yiddish theatre, and I am neither referring to or defending the elocutionary high-style. Blanche Yurka in Classical drama, Katina Paxinou's animal outcries of grief in the otherwise farcical film, *Mourning Becomes Electra,* Peter Lorre's grinding falsettos, Anton Walbrook's broken-voiced speech before the curtain, in *Red Shoes*: the popular aversion to these strenuous displays of feeling is less than a rational distaste for an art démodé; it is fear of vitality. In his projection of strong emotion, the "natural man," with few regional exceptions, uncalculatedly brings into operation a distinct physical style, determined by factors of his physique, his occupation, and his social conditioning. Any crisis-acting not founded on the re-creation of such emotion and such style, skillfully heightened, is inadequate to its source. But a population grown effete finds the shallow-breathing Olivier, for glaring example, a suitable vehicle of tragic feeling. Toshiro Mifune, the bandit of *Rashomon* (a soldier whom Kurosawa "discovered," and then *Kabuki*-trained), has more kinesis in his feet—literally in his feet!—than Olivier has in his entire body.

I have not elaborated these details for the sole purpose of out-flanking the cognoscenti. I think it advisable for the unprepared at-tender to Japanese films to beware of the footnoters before he has assimilated his own unguarded experience, and to discriminate for himself between what is deeply universal in these films and what is special to them. Further considerations of decor, lighting, of color, histrionic subtleties, and so on will present themselves for analysis when we have seen not only *Musashi* but also *The Tale of Genji*, *The Life of Oharu*, *Seven Samurai*, and *A Women's Life*, all period pieces. The extent to which we have been charmed by costume films will be tested when we have seen the best of Japan's films on con-temporary subjects, which will probably be a long time off. That these will pass the test there seems little question, judging by reports on such films as Kurosawa's *To Live* or *Drunken Angel*. We consider Kurosawa a man apart, but many Japanese critics will not have it so and assure us that directors whose work we've seen no samples of are equally significant. We await the evidence. Meanwhile, on the evi-dence available and beyond the reservations of the experts, we can acknowledge that the heart of the Japanese film is animated from below the luminous surface. No matter what contingencies of the world market Daiei productions have been designed to meet, they have touched—above all, in *Rashomon*—the deepest and most im-placable concerns of man, with cinematic values unmatched by any present body of filmmakers, possibly excepting the Swedish.

# Memory of Defeat in Japan:
# A Reappraisal of RASHOMON
## by JAMES F. DAVIDSON

The signing of the military-aid pact between the United States and Japan early this year formally marked the opening of a new phase in the relationship between the two countries and an end to the interlude of the "Switzerland of the Pacific." It signified the American desire to see the country so recently known as a defeated enemy and devastated dependent become an increasingly self-sufficient and dependable ally.

Outcroppings of anti-Americanism in Japan since the end of the occupation have been of the type that could be expected in the period of readjustment, with the Japanese reactions to the hydrogen bomb tests adding a special sort of tension. The underlying attitudes are the real point of concern, and these should have more attention in the future than Americans have been accustomed over the past few years to give to Japanese opinion. The attitude of an ally both deserves and requires a different quality of understanding than is accorded to a subdued enemy.

As a particular insight into Japanese feelings, it is worth taking another look at the most widely acclaimed of Japan's dramatic products since the war, the origin of which dates well back into the occupation period. It is now more than two years since the film

*From* The Antioch Review *14, no. 4 (December 1954). Copyright* © *1954 by* The Antioch Review. *Reprinted by permission of the publisher.*

*Rashomon* was first seen by New York audiences after having won the Grand Prize at the International Film Festival in Venice. It was subsequently shown in many American cities and won critics' citations as an outstanding foreign film. The purpose of this review is to point out some implications of *Rashomon* in terms of the Japanese reflection on their defeat and occupation which were completely overlooked by American reviews at the time. These overtones are present throughout the picture and come through strongly in many of its details. Without producing a consistent theme, they heighten the dramatic effect of the story upon a Japanese audience in a way which is easily lost upon the foreign observer.

The story is laid in the ancient capitol of Kyoto, during a troubled period in the ninth century. It concerns a samurai and his wife waylaid on the road by a notorious bandit. The man is killed and the woman flees, later seeking refuge in a temple whence she is brought to the police magistrate after the capture of the bandit. A woodcutter who found the body and a Buddhist priest who passed the couple on the day of the crime are present at the testimony. As the picture opens, these two relate the events to a stranger while the three seek shelter from the rain in the ruins of the great gate of Kyoto, the Rashomon.

The bandit, Tajomaru, boasted that he had slain the man. Catching a glimpse of the woman as the couple passed him on the road, he had resolved to possess her, and, if possible, to do so without killing her husband. With a tale of swords and mirrors buried near an abandoned temple, he enticed the man into the woods, where he overcame and bound him. On being led to the spot, the wife attacked the bandit with a dagger, fighting like a tigress until at last, exhausted and hysterical, she not only succumbed but finally returned his embrace.

Afterwards, as he was about to leave, she stopped him, saying that she could not stand disgrace in the eyes of two men. One must die, and she belong to the other. He released the husband and they fought. After the samurai had won the bandit's admiration by crossing swords with him longer than any previous foe, he was slain. Finding the woman gone, the bandit took the horse and weapons, except for the dagger, which he forgot. He was apprehended shortly after, writhing ignominiously with stomach cramps as a result of drinking from a polluted stream.

According to the wife, the bandit left after the attack, laughing derisively. She ran to her husband to find nothing but contempt in his eyes, even when she cut his ropes and begged him to kill her. Maddened by his stare, she approached with the dagger, fainted, and recovered to find that she had plunged it into his chest.

Next, in a procedure which modern homicide squads must contemplate wistfully, the testimony of the dead man is obtained through a medium. He says that the bandit urged his wife to go with him, declaring his love and saying that her husband would not want her now. To his horror, she not only consented, but as they left she pulled the bandit back and cried, "Kill him!" The bandit stared at her in unbelief and then said to her husband, "Shall we kill her, or let her go? You decide." For that, says the dead man, he could almost forgive him. As he hesitated, she wrenched free and fled. After a chase, the bandit returned alone, cut his ropes, and left. He rose, sobbing, found the dagger and killed himself. As he lost consciousness, he was aware of someone approaching and drawing out the dagger.

At this point in the film, the stranger laughs at the discomfort of the two narrators. The priest is miserable because the same faith that requires him to believe the dead man's story is shaken by the account of the woman's treachery. The woodcutter suddenly bursts out that he knows the man was killed with a sword because he saw it happen. He concealed his knowledge from the police out of a desire not to be involved. Coming upon the clearing, he had seen the man bound and the bandit entreating the woman. Finally, she ran to her husband, cut his ropes, and threw herself on the ground halfway between the men. The bandit drew, but the husband refused to risk his life for her, saying, "I regret the loss of my horse more." The bandit considered a moment, then turned to leave and rebuffed the woman as she ran after him.

She began to laugh wildly and denounced both of them. She had long been sick of "this farce," indicating her husband, and had been thrilled to learn the identity of her attacker. Perhaps Tajomaru was a way out for her. But no! He did not take her like a conqueror. She told her husband that he could hardly sneer at her honor if he was too poor a specimen to fight for her. Goaded by her, they fought unwillingly, unskillfully, even cravenly. It was not a duel; it was a terrified brawl. At last the husband was trapped in the undergrowth and, shouting that he did not want to die, was run through. The staggering, painting Tajomaru returned to the woman, who had watched in horrified fascination. She fought him off and fled. He then gathered up both swords and left.

When the woodcutter has finished his account, the stranger again laughs at the unhappiness of the other two over this exposure of human frailty and deceit. "Men want to forget things they don't like," he says. These three now become principals in the epilogue, which is very important to an understanding of the film. They hear a cry and discover an abandoned baby around a corner of the gate. The stranger, who reaches it first, strips the blankets from it. The horrified priest takes the baby while the woodcutter seizes the stranger and denounces him as the incarnation of evil. He justifies himself, saying that the parents have abandoned their duty and he is not obliged to take it up. Everyone must live any way he can, and if he does not steal the blankets someone else will. Still pressed by the woodcutter, he rebounds with the taunt that he knows why the last story was concealed from the police. He accuses the woodcutter of having taken the dagger, described by the bandit as valuable, from the scene of the crime. The crestfallen woodcutter makes no denial, and the stranger dashes off into the rain with the blankets, jeering.

The two stand in silence. Then the woodcutter takes the child, saying that he has six and one more will make little difference. The priest thanks him for restoring his faith in man and, as the sky clears, watches him proceed homeward from the steps of the gate.

Not all American critics were favorably impressed with *Rashomon*. Even reviews that praised it contained adjectives such as "slow," "repetitious," "humorlessly solemn," and "confused." The extravagance of the acting was much remarked. Two reviewers, from their mutually distant corners in *Time* and the *New Republic*, singled out the sentimental epilogue as a serious flaw, arbitrarily and unfitly added. It was duly noted that the film draws from the works of the brilliant author Ryunosuke Akutagawa, who committed suicide in 1927 at the age of thirty-five. The basis, however, was not a novel was widely reported, but two short stories. The stories are completely separate, and the scenarist-director, Akira Kurosawa, combined them into a product considerably different from either. The original stories therefore throw some light on the central problem of the film.

The first story, *Yabu no Naka*,[1] supplied the basic plot: the conflicting accounts of the same crime by those involved. Akutagawa took an old melodrama and, with the clever detachment for which he is famous, made it ask Pilate's question. The circumstances presented as actual are essentially the same as in the film. Then there are the confessions of the bandit, the wife, and the dead man. That is all. There is no fourth account by an eye witness, no comment on the implications of the testimonies.

The second story, *Rashomon,* in addition to the title, contributed the setting, atmosphere, and the idea of characters who discuss right and wrong, duty and necessity. Kyoto has been devastated by a series of natural calamities: earthquakes, whirlwinds, and fires. The Rashomon has fallen into decay and become a hideout for thieves and a depository for unclaimed corpses. A servant of a samurai, just discharged because of hard times, seeks its shelter from the rain. He contemplates the gloomy surroundings and his gloomy prospects, and debates with himself whether or not to become a thief. Climbing the stairs to the tower to find a corner for the night, he comes upon an old woman among the corpses, pulling the hair from one. He seizes her and demands to know what she is doing. She explains that she takes the hair for a wig. The dead woman used to sell snake meat as fish. If she knew the other had to take her hair to live, she probably wouldn't care. Listening, the man makes the decision he could not, earlier. Tearing off the hag's clothes and throwing her down among the corpses, he runs into the night.

Why was an atmosphere of gloom and decay, of physical and spir-

---

[1] "In a Grove." All comments on the original stories refer to *Rashomon and Other Stories,* tr. Takashi Kojima (New York: Liveright, 1952).

itual misery, chosen as a background in the film? The original story of the crime contains no such atmosphere, no linking of the event to the conditions of the times. Its effect is all the more striking because of this. If the sole aim of the film was to depict individual lust, self-ishness and falsehood as a timeless problem, as favorable American reviews acclaimed, then it could well have been more faithful to the spirit, as well as the words, of Akutagawa in developing the remark-able event in less remarkable circumstances. It should not be for-gotten that this film was made in the first instance for Japanese audiences, at a time when Japanese films were only beginning to emerge from an understandable period of complete escapism. A drama laid in medieval Japan, involving questions of human nature, could have provided a respectable type of escape without sacrificing its integrity. Yet the picure opens on the ruined Rashomon: once the great architectural symbol of the capital of Japan, now the crum-bling reflection of a devastated city whence the seat of power has moved. It is deluged by a relentless, windless rain. Under the gate sit the priest and the woodcutter, exchanging mute glances and head-shakes. The priest slowly recites the kinds of disaster that have be-fallen. "And now this. I may lose my faith." Later, shrugging off their story, the stranger says, "Who is honest nowadays, anyway?" It is hard to believe that a Japanese audience was not being led to refer to their own experience and to see the events of the story accordingly.

The man and wife are depicted at the outset as the very embodi-ment of Japanese virtue, refinement, and prosperity. He is a samurai, of the ancient warrior caste whose tradition was so carefully pre-served until 1945; handsome, weaponed and well dressed. As they pass the priest, he turns and laughs happily up at his wife. She is mounted on a fine horse and veiled from view. Lovely and petite, she seemed to the bandit in that first glance, he says, like an angel.

The bandit, as portrayed in the film, is a most remarkable char-acter. In the original story, he wears a blue silk kimono and joins the couple as a traveling companion in order to divert them from the road with talk of buried treasure. There is evidently nothing un-usual in his appearance or manner, and he easily disguises his iden-tity and intentions so as to be acceptable. The film Tajomaru, on the other hand, is a half-clad savage, uncouth, insolent, and raucous, who "capers about the screen," as the London *Times* said, "like a ferocious, demented Puck following with maniacal laughter." He appears the least Japanese of all the characters, and a sort of incarnation of the *oni,* or ogre, of Japanese folklore, which has often been interpreted as a representation of the foreigner. His build and movements, even his features, suggest something of the gangling awkwardness that appears in Japanese caricatures of Occidentals. He is alternately terrifying and ridiculous, but always alien to the others. This serves to emphasize the avariciousness and foolishness of the samurai who, significantly, leaves his wife and undertakes the journey to his ruin as a commercial venture.

The scene in which the wife is overcome in a prolonged kiss (in itself still a shocker for Japanese audiences) is more horrifying because her attacker is a sweating, scratching, bug-slapping barbarian than it would have been with Akutagawa's blue-kimonoed outlaw. The strong suggestion of cultural difference, verging on the ethnic, gives her ultimate lustful response an additional meaning. The problem is as old as conquest. And the epilogue of the abandoned child takes on a practical significance which removes from it much of the stigma of artistic error which it must bear if considered only as a disconnected attempt to restore fish in goodness.

In the original story, the wife tells her husband very simply that she cannot live with her disgrace and his contempt, and that she cannot leave him alive as a witness to them. Then she kills him, but fails in her attempt to kill herself. In the film, her confession is, in effect, a plea of temporary insanity. While she does not admit to any guilt in yielding to the bandit, nothing is done to remove the impression made by the scene which shows her to the audience as finally sharing his passion. She sobs hysterically and concludes her story by beseeching the audience—which sits in the position of the judge throughout the testimonies— "But what could I, a poor woman, do?"

The woodcutter, in the original story simply a witness who found the body, becomes an eyewitness whose account provides a devastating contrast to the others. Yet in the end he, too, is implicated, and the truth again eludes the others. Aside from his story, he has a place in the commentary and the epilogue as one of the only two commoners in the picture. The other is the stranger, who accepts human depravity with a laugh, jeers at the struggles of those who would deny it, and makes what he can for himself without scruple. The woodcutter is a simple man, striving to be honest under the burden of a large family and hard times. He is disturbed by a sense of his own guilt and the knowledge of the guilt of the other three. The priest, with less knowledge of the event than the other, shares his feeling with even greater unhappiness, for he perceives its fatal consequences for his faith.

The *Times,* more perspicacious in its perplexity over *Rashomon* than the American accolades, notes that there is little ritual about it and that even the music does not seem to be distinctively Japanese. This touches an important point about the epilogue. The picture has been filled with noise and confusion. Aside from the hysterics of the woman, much of the noise has been the derisive laughter of the bandit and the cynical stranger: the laughter which, even in silence, rings in the ears of a proud man defeated and reduced. There is practically no ritual and all reminders of contemporary Japan are unpleasant. Then, as the woodcutter takes the baby from the priest and goes home, both bow twice, ceremoniously. The priest stands on the steps of the Rashomon, which no longer looks so ruined in the emerging sunlight. The music has suddenly become traditional. The final act of grace has restored a particularly Japanese kind of rightness.

There is a striking similarity with a final scene in *The Well-Digger's Daughter,* where the unmarried mother, the repentant father, and the grandparents, separated by social barriers, are united around the crib of the baby. Raimu, as the well-digger, has a speech in which he urges that the past be forgotten in love for the child. "For here," he says, "is our hope. Here is France." The French in 1946 had need of a hope in which to sink the bitter divisions of the past. Postwar Japan is in need of a belief on which to found a duty. Surely the epilogue of *Rashomon* points, after the unanswerable questions raised in the story, to a basic belief and duty for Japanese to hold to. The old vision of a hopeful future springing from a glorious past is lost, and the way to its recovery lies through a maze of doubtful thoughts about misfortune, guilt, and shame. Yet there is a new Japan, which demands love and care, like the abandoned child, not because of its auspicious or legitimate beginnings, but because it is alive and will perish without them.

It would be foolish to argue that the film is a complete or consistent allegory. To refer again to the *Times* review, however, ". . . something, some part of a country's habits of thinking, some perhaps unconscious reflection of its prejudices and preferences, filters through the lens of the camera to perplex or amuse the foreigner." Much of the perplexity can be avoided by recognizing the implications for the Japanese audience, intermediate beween the basic story and the more universal meaning. These aid the story in supporting the commentary, and fill the picture in spots that would otherwise be empty. They also help to account for the unrestrained, un-Oriental acting. The actors are portraying emotions which Japanese are conditioned by recent events to feel strongly, and their portrayals must be adequate to these feelings as well as to the events of the story. In these terms, even the agonized contortions of the medium as she establishes contact with the spirit of the dead samurai seem to have some meaning.

*Rashomon* was not popular in Japan on its first showing, although there has been more interest in a second circulation since its international awards. It is not a popular-type production, but many circles there have received it enthusiastically. Without substantiating the specific arguments of this review, a prominent Japanese official assured the writer that the significance for the current situation in Japan was widely accepted. Any full understanding of the film, he added, must consider it in terms of the current feelings of Japanese.

The story told by each of the three participants protects his self-respect. In the account of the woodcutter, the common man, they are all revealed as frauds. The fight is a travesty on that described by the bandit, after which the mighty Tajomaru, heaving with fright and exertion, goes off to be betrayed into capture by a rebellion of his own innards. Bitter satire on the heroic virtues finds a natural response in a defeated nation. Still, we are reminded, the woodcutter also has a motive for changing the facts to conceal his guilt.

How did the old beliefs and loyalties die? Did they perish in a defeat at arms which "liberated" those who had already begun to see through them? Did they, in a manner of speaking, annihilate themselves in shame and sorrow for a people no longer worthy of them? Were they destroyed by those who held them dear because they were an unbearable reminder of duties that could no longer be fulfilled? Or were they done in in an uncertain scuffle of ideals and proclamations and conflicting directives that left nothing firm and whole in their place? Finally, since ideals do not die as men die, the question remains, Are they really dead? It seems unlikely that thoughtful Japanese would see *Rashomon* without having some of these questions brought to mind. Even small touches may strike a chord. For example, when the bandit pleads with the woman to go with him and then, impatient at getting no reply, shakes her roughly and shouts, "Say yes, will you!" some might see something of the ambivalent attitude of SCAP.

Just how intentionally Kurosawa worked these overtones into his film is questionable. Since he has taught us so well that the confession of a principal may be a poor guide to truth, perhaps we shall never know. However that may be, he produced an amazing work in *Rashomon* and, despite its roughness, a great motion picture. If the implications for Japanese are those here described, they carry little self-pity and have the same objective balancing of error and guilt into an open question as the rest of the film. This is what makes the solution of the epilogue particularly touching. As an artistic achievement and as a searching of the soul, *Rashomon* is something of which any country could be proud. What it may signify for future developments in Japan, and for relations with the United States, remains to be seen.

# RASHOMON as Modern Art

## by PARKER TYLER

*Rashomon,* the Japanese film masterpiece, is a story about a double crime: rape and homicide (or possibly suicide). The time is the eighth century A.D. It is told in retrospect, and in successive layers, by the three participants, the dead warrior (through a mediumistic priestess), his raped wife, and a notorious bandit perhaps responsible for the warrior's death as well as for his wife's violation, and by a woodcutter who alleges himself to have witnessed, accidentally, the whole episode. The quality of the film narrative is so fine that an astonishingly unified effect emerges from the conflicting stories furnished by the three principals and (following the inquest) by the lone witness. The bandit and the woman have separately fled the scene of the crimes, where the woodcutter claims, at first, to have arrived only in time to find the warrior's corpse. Nominally, the film comes under the familiar heading of stories that reconstruct crimes. However, this story does not go much beyond the presentation of each person's testimony.

The woman claims to have killed her husband in an irresponsible fit of horror after the rape took place; her husband claims to have committed hara-kiri out of grief and humiliation; the bandit claims to have killed him in honorable combat; and the woodcutter confirms the bandit's story while picturing the conduct of all participants quite differently from the ways they respectively describe it.

*From* Three Faces of the Film *by Parker Tyler (Cranbury, N.J.: A. S. Barnes & Company, Inc., 1967). Reprinted by permission of the author and the publisher. This article originally appeared in* Cinema 16 *(1952).*

As no trial of either of the living participants is shown, and as no consequent action reveals anything conclusive as to the crime, the decision as to the actual truth of the whole affair falls to the spectator's option. Since technically the woodcutter is the only "objective" witness, he might seem the most reliable of the four testifiers. But his integrity is *not* beyond question; the version by the warrior's ghost has contradicted his version in an important detail— one inadvertently confirmed by the woodcutter's implicit admission (in an incident following the inquest) that he stole a dagger at the scene of the crime. The ghost has testified that he felt "someone" draw from his breast the dagger with which he alleges he committed hara-kiri.

Logically, if one's aim be to establish in theory the "legal" truth of the affair, the only obvious method is to correlate all the admissible facts of the action with the four persons involved, in order to determine their relative integrity as individuals—a procedure complicated necessarily not merely by the given criminal status of one participant but by the fact that all but the woodcutter have willingly assumed guilt. A further difficulty, in general, is that nothing of the background of any character is given beyond what can be assumed from his visible behavior and his social status; for example, there is only the merest hint of something unusual in the journey of the warrior and his lady through the forest. Again, even from direct observation, we have to depend a great deal on these persons as seen through the eyes of each other. So, unless one be prejudiced for one sex or another, one social class or another, it seems almost impossible to make a really plausible choice of the truth-teller (if any). Are we to conclude, in this dilemma, that *Rashomon* amounts to no more than a trick piece, a conventional mystery melodrama, left hanging? My answer is *No.* There are several things about the movie which argue it as a unique and conscious art, the opposite of a puzzle; or at least, no more of a puzzle than those modern paintings of which a spectator may be heard to say, "But what is it? What is it supposed to mean?"

Perhaps more than one profane critic has wisecracked of a Picasso, a Dali, or an Ernst, that it demands, *a posteriori,* the method described by the police as "the reconstruction of the crime." My opinion is that the last thing required for the elucidation of *Rashomon*'s mystery is something corresponding to a jury's verdict. Such a judgment, aesthetically speaking, is as inutile for appreciating the substance of this movie as for appreciating the art of Picasso. In *Rashomon*, there is no strategic effort to conceal any more than a modern painter's purpose is to conceal instead of reveal. The basic issue, in art, must always be *what* the creator desires to reveal. Of such a painting as Picasso's *Girl Before Mirror*, it may be said that it contains an "enigma." But this enigma is merely one specific aspect of the whole mystery of being, a particular insight into human consciousness in terms of the individual, and so has that complex poetry of which all profound art partakes. So with the enigma of *Rashomon*. This great Japanese film is a "mystery story" to the extent that existence itself is a mystery, as conceived in the deepest psychological and aesthetic senses. As applied to a movie of this class, however, such a theory is certainly unfamiliar and therefore has to be explained.

Chagall with his levitated fantasy-world and childhood symbols, Picasso with his creative analysis of psychological movements translated into pictorial vision—such painters set forth *nude* mysteries of human experience; each, in the static field of the painting, reveals multiple aspects of a single reality, whether literally or in symbols. *Rashomon*, as a time art, cinema, corresponds with multiple-image painting as a space art. The simplest rendering of time phases in an object within the unilateral space of a single picture is, of course, in Futurist painting, such as Balla's famous dog, ambling by the moving skirts of its owner; the dachshund's legs are portrayed multiply with a fanlike, flickering kind of image similar to images as seen in the old-fashioned "bioscope" movie machine. The same dynamic principle was illustrated by Muybridge's original time-photography of a running horse, except that the register there was not instantaneous but successive; at least, the photographer had the cinematic idea of keeping pace with a running horse to show the pendulumlike span of its front and hind legs while its body seemed to stay in the same place (treadmill dynamics). Even in the contemporary movie camera, some movements may be so fast that one gets the sort of blur shown in Futurist images. The analogy of

*Rashomon* with such procedures of stating physical movement is that, for the single action photographed, a complex action (or "episode") is substituted, and for the single viewpoint toward this action, multiple (and successive) viewpoints. The camera in this movie is actually trained four times on what theoretically is the same episode; if the results are different each time, it is because each time the camera represents the viewpoint of a different person; a viewpoint mainly different, of course, not because of the physical angle (the camera is never meant to substitute for subjective vision) but because of the psychological angle.

"Simultaneous montage" in cinema is the double exposure of two views so that multiple actions occur in a *unilateral space visually* while existing in *separate spaces literally* and possibly—as when a person and his visual recollection are superimposed on the same film frame—also in separate times. A remarkable aspect of the method of depicting memory in *Rashomon* is its simplicity: Each person, squatting in Japanese fashion as he testifies, squarely faces the camera and speaks; then, rather than simultaneous montage, a flashback takes place: the scene shifts wholly to the fatal spot in the forest. The police magistrate is never shown and no questions addressed to the witnesses are heard. When it is the dead man's turn to testify, the priestess performs the required rite, becomes possessed by his spirit, speaks in his voice, and the scene shifts back as in the other cases. Thus we receive the successive versions of the action with little intervention between them and with the minimum of "courtroom action."

Of course, there is a framing story, which retrospectively reveals the inquest itself. The action literally begins at the Rashomon Gate, a great ruin where the woodcutter and the priest, who has previously seen the woman and been present at the inquest, are sheltered during a rainstorm; joined by a tramp, these two gradually reveal everything that has taken place according to the several versions. What is important is the inherent value of the way the technique of the flashback has been variously used. The separate stories are equally straightforward, equally forceful; no matter which version is being related, his own or another's, every participant behaves with the same conviction. As a result (it was certainly this specta-

tor's experience), one is compelled to believe each story implicitly
as it unfolds, and oddly none seems to cancel another out. Therefore it would be only from the policeman's viewpoint of wanting to
pin guilt on one of the persons that, ultimately, any obligation
would be felt to sift the conflicting evidence and render a formal
verdict. Despite the incidental category of its form, *Rashomon* as a
work of art naturally seems to call for a response having nothing
to do with a courtroom.

Of an event less significant, less stark and rudimentary in terms
of human behavior, the technical question of "the truth" might
prove insistent enough to embarrass one's judgment. The inevitable
impulse, at first sight, is to speculate on which of those who claim
guilt is really guilty of the warrior's death. But whatever conclusion
be tentatively reached, what eventually slips back into the spectator's mind and possesses it is the traumatic violence of the basic
pattern: that violence which is the heart of the enigma. The civilization of this medieval period is turned topsy-turvy by the bandit's
strategy, in which he tricks the man, ties him up, and forces him to
witness his wife's violation. It is only from this point forward that
the stories differ: the woman's reaction to the bandit's assault, the
husband's behavior after being freed from his bonds—everything is
disputed by one version or another. But is not the heart of the confusion *within the event itself?* Is this happening not one so fright-
fully destructive of human poise and ethical custom that it breeds
its own ambiguity, and that this ambiguity infects the minds of
these people?

All the participants are suffering from shock: the warrior's agonized ghost, his hysterical wife, the bandit, when caught, seized with
mad bravado. Unexpectedly—for the paths of the couple and the
bandit have crossed purely by accident—three lives have been irre-
trievably altered after being reduced to the most primitive condition conceivable. Two men (in a manner in which, at best, etiquette
has only a vestigial role) have risked death for the possession of a
woman. Basically, it is a pattern that was born with the beginnings
of mankind. Such an event, in civilized times of high culture, would
of itself contain something opaque and even incredible. What matters morally is not how, from moment to moment, the affair was

played out by its actors but that it should have been played *at all*. The illicit impulse springing up in the bandit's breast as the lady's long veil blows aside is so violent that its consequences attack the sense of reality as its moral root. Regardless of what literally took place in the forest's depths that mild summer day, each participant is justified in reconstructing it in a manner to redeem the prestige of the moral sense, which, consciously or not, is a civilized person's most precious possession. It should be emphasized that it is the Japanese people who are involved, and that to them honor is of peculiarly paramount value; even the bandit is quick to seize the opportunity to maintain—truthfully or not—that he behaved like a man of caste rather than an outlaw; he has testified that following the rape (to which, he says, the woman yielded willingly) he untied the husband and worsted him in fair swordplay.

Hence, a psychologically unilateral, indisputable perspective exists in which the tragic episode can be viewed *by the spectator:* a perspective contrary to that in which one of the persons appears technically guilty of the warrior's death. This perspective is simply the catastrophe as a single movement which temporarily annihilated the moral reality on which civilized human consciousness is based. The "legal" or objective reality of the affair (what might be called its *statistics*) is exactly what cannot be recovered, because the physical episode, as human action, has been *self-annihilating*. Of course, then, it might be claimed that the woodcutter, not being involved except as a spectator, is a disinterested witness of the episode, and accordingly his story that the three actors in the tragedy really played a grim farce, in which two cowards were the heroes and a shrew the heroine, is the correct version. But the opening scene of the framing story makes it plain that the woodcutter's mind is in a state similar to that of the participants themselves; indeed, he is evidently dismayed and apparently by the fact that all their testimony belies what he proceeds to reveal to the priest and the tramp as "the truth." However, as the shocked witness of such a debacle of the social order—in any case a victory of evil over good—this peasant may have withheld his testimony out of superstitious timidity. If, in fact, he saw all that took place, then the added confusion that the participants contradict each other may raise bewilderment in his simple mind—may even tempt him to exploit his subconscious envy and resentment against his betters by imagining their behavior as disgraceful and ludicrous. It seems within *Rashomon*'s subtle pattern to suggest that even a simple, disinterested witness should be drawn psychologically into the chaos of this incident; after all, there is no proof that he did not invent his own account in competition with the others'. This assumption would lend credit to the conclusion that the real function of each witness's story is to salvage his own sense of reality, however close his version to the event as it took place. Perhaps it would be accurate to add that the facts themselves have no true legal status, since each witness is forced to draw on his subjective imagination rather than on his capacity to observe. In this case, each is in the position of the proto-artist, who uses reality only as a crude norm; the sense of invention enters *into* reality. On the other hand, there is the literal truth of the denouement, the climax of the framing story, in which the woodcutter adopts a foundling baby who has been left in the Gate's interior. The relation of this incident to the story proper strikes me as the most problematical element of all, if only because the film would have remained intact without it.

Morally, of course, this incident functions as a reinstatement of human values in the sense of good. But the specifically religious view that humanity has hopelessly degraded itself in the forest episode (the view represented by the priest) is more external than essential to the whole conception. The priest thinks in terms equivalent, logically, to the law's terms: truth or falsehood. Since some lying is self-evident, the sin of concealment is added to crime; i.e., concealment of the truth, not of the crime, for all profess crime. Ironically enough, *confession* has become a sin. What seems significant to the whole is the collective nature of the liars: they literally outnumber the truth-teller (whichever he may be). The "sin" involved has gone beyond individual performance and exists objectively, as would a natural cataclysm such as a volcanic eruption. That each participant assumes guilt, including the dead man, reveals the comprehensiveness and irresistibility of the disorder. A lie, then, actually becomes the symbol of the operation by which these people mutually regain their moral identities. These identities having been destroyed as though by an objective force beyond anyone's control, any means seems fair to regain them. Since, however, they cannot separate themselves from the sense of *tragedy,* they prefer to be tragedy's heroes—its animating will rather than its passive objects. But why should the three tragedies seem as one?

To revert to our analogy with the visual media of painting and still photography, the plastic reality with which we have to deal in *Rashomon* is multiform rather than uniform. Within one span of time-and-space, reality (the episode in the forest) has been disintegrated. While the witnesses' stories accomplish its reintegration, they do not do so in terms of the *physically unilateral* except in the final aesthetic sense in which the totality of a work exists all at once in a spectator's mind. The analogy is complex, but literally it is with the Futuristic image of the walking dog; like this image, the total image of *Rashomon* varies only in detail and degree. There is no variation on the background and origin of the tragedy; no contradiction as to the main physical patterns of the rape and the death of the warrior by a blade wound. So the main visual aspect is held firmly, unilaterally, in place. Another image of Futurist painting renders the angles of air displacement caused by the nose of a racing auto. Such "displacements" exist in *Rashomon* severally in the respective accounts of a physical action deriving from one main impetus: the desire to possess a woman.

The total psychological space in this movie, because of its complexity, is rendered in literal time as is music. A similar psychological space is rendered *simultaneously* in Picasso's *Girl Before Mirror* by the device of the mirror as well as by the double image of profile-and-fullface on the girl. Her moonlike face has a symbolic integralness as different "phases" of the same person; that is, her fullface denotes her personality as it confronts the world and her profile her personality as it confronts itself: the mirror image in which the fullface character of her aspect is diminished. To Meyer Schapiro we owe a basic observation as to this painting: It plays specifically on the body-image which each individual has of himself and others, and which is distinct from the anatomical image peculiarly available to photography. The mirror image in Picasso's work thus asserts a psychological datum parallel with the dominantly subjective testimony of each witness in *Rashomon's* tragedy. The mirror of the movie screen is like the mirror in the painting as telescoped within the image of the total painting; successively, we see people as they think of themselves and as they are to others; for example, at one point during the woman's story, the camera substitutes for the viewpoint of her husband toward whom she lifts a dagger: We see her as conceived by herself but also as she would have been in her husband's eyes. In revealing, with such expressiveness and conviction, what novels have often revealed through first-person narratives or the interior monologue, the film necessarily emphasizes its *visual* significance. The sum of these narratives in *Rashomon* rests on the elements of the tragedy in which all agree: One raped, one was raped, one killed, one was killed. The "variations" are accountable through something which I would place parallel with Schapiro's body-image concept: the *psychic image* that would apply especially to the memory of a past event in which the body-image is charged with maintaining, above all, its moral integrity, its ideal dignity. In a sense, Picasso's girl reconstructs and synthesizes her outer self-divisions within the depths of the mirror; so in the depths of each person's memory, in *Rashomon,* is recreated the image of what took place far away in the forest as consistent with his ideal image of himself.

In modern times, the human personality—as outstandingly demonstrated in the tragicomedies of Pirandello—is easily divided against itself. But what makes a technically schizophrenic situation important and dramatically interesting is, paradoxically, the individual's sense of his former or possible unity, for without this sense he would not struggle morally against division: he would be satisfied to be "more than one person." In analytical cubism, we have a pictorial style expressing an ironic situation within the human individual's total physique, including his clothes; we do not perceive, within an individual portrayed by Picasso in this manner, a moral "split" or psychological "confusion"; rather we see the subject's phenomenal appearance portrayed formalistically in terms of its internal or "depth" elements, its overlaid facets, or complex layers of being, which—though presumably not meant to signify a conflict in the personality—correspond logically, nevertheless, to the moral dialectic within all consciousness (subjective/objective, personal/social, and so on). The same logical correspondence is seen even more plainly in the anatomical dialectic of Tchelitchew's recent paintings, where the separate inner systems are seen in labyrinthine relation to the skin surface. Indeed, man as an internal labyrinth is common to diverse styles of modern painting, all such styles necessarily implying, as human statements, the sometimes bewildering complexity of man's spiritual being. Great beauty is justifiably found in such aesthetic forms, which indirectly symbolize an ultimate mystery: that *human* mystery to which *Rashomon* so eloquently testifies in its own way and which comprises the transition from birth to death, from the organic to the inorganic, which is the individual's necessary material fate.

Against the awareness of his material fate, the individual erects many defenses: art, pleasure, ethics, God, religion, immortality—ideas, sensations, and acts whose continuity in him are preserved by constant cultivation, periodic renewal, unconscious "testimony." These constitute his moral identity in the social order. In them resides the essence of his being, the law of his contentment (such as it be), and his rational ability to function from hour to hour. In the lives of the persons of *Rashomon,* where this objective order prevailed, utter chaos was suddenly injected. Each person was shaken out of himself, became part of that blind flux which joins the intuition of the suspense-before-birth with that of the suspense-before-death and whose name is terror. This was largely because of the tragedy's physical violence, which temporarily vanquished human reason. If we look at the terror of war as depicted in Picasso's *Guernica,* we observe a social cataclysm of which the forest episode in *Rashomon* is a microcosm. Curiously enough, *Guernica* happens to be divided vertically into four main sections, or panels, which Picasso has subtly unified by overlapping certain formal elements. Thus, while the great massacre is of course highly simplified here in visual terms, it is moreover synthesized by means of four stages or views. As wrenched by violence as are the individual forms, they congregate, so to speak, to make order out of confusion. Though Picasso was not recomposing from memory, he might have been; in any case, the drive of art is toward formal order, and the individuals in *Rashomon,* as proto-artists, have this same drive. As gradually accumulated, the sum total of *Rashomon* constitutes a *time mural* whose unity lies in the fact that, however different are the imaginations of the four witnesses, whatever harsh vibrations their mutual contradictions set up, the general design (as the filmmakers have molded it) remains and dominates the work's final aspect of great beauty and great truth.

# Plot Synopsis

*Rashomon* is a collection of versions of the truth about an attack, a rape, and a robbery, all of which occurred during the Middle Ages in the old Japanese capital of Kyoto, then called Miyako. These stories are being discussed by three people—a woodcutter, a commoner, and a priest—at the gate, Rashomon, where the three have gathered to shelter themselves from the rain.

They recount the various versions. The woodcutter says originally that he merely found some articles at the scene of the crime. He then relates the story that he heard the bandit, Tajomaru, tell the magistrate. The bandit said he had tied up the samurai husband and tried to rape the wife, only to find that she was quite ready to give in to him. Later, however, he said he had been forced (by the unfaithful wife) to fight with the husband, and he had won.

The priest next gives the version that he heard the wife tell the magistrate. It is quite different. She said that after she had given herself to the bandit her husband hated her, and, distraught, she had killed him herself.

The next version is probably told by the priest. It concerns the dead man's story, told through the lips of a medium called in by the magistrate. It too is different from the others. The samurai said that after the seduction his wife had tried to have the bandit murder him. In this she had failed, but he had killed himself with a dagger.

At this point the woodcutter is made to confess that he did not tell the whole truth, nor did he complete his story. He says that the husband indeed no longer respected his wife. She, in fury, goaded the two men into fighting and the husband was killed. She fled from the bandit. He was left alone and eventually captured.

The three comment upon these various stories. Unaccounted for in any of them are the murder weapons. The bandit had said that the sword was sold; and the dagger is also missing. An amount of suspicion falls naturally upon the woodcutter, who had not told his whole story the first time, and the suspicion of theft is deepened by the possibility of murder.

None of this is resolved, however. The three are distracted by the cry of an infant abandoned in the attic of the old gate. The commoner wants to strip it and sell its clothes. The woodcutter takes pity upon it and, although he has hungry children of his own, decides to take it home. The priest, who has been speaking of the sinfulness of the times, is reassured, his faith in man returned. The rain ceases and the sun appears. The three, one by one, leave the great gate that sheltered them.

# Content Outline

Title sequence leading directly into first scene at the gate, and discussion among the woodcutter, priest, commoner, ending with first story of the woodcutter.

The woodcutter in the forest finds the woman's hat and veil, then the corpse of the husband.

The woodcutter at the magistrate's, telling what he found.

The priest at the magistrate's, affirming that he saw the murdered man three days before.

The scene itself, as described by the priest.

The priest concluding his evidence at the magistrate's.

The police agent at the magistrate's, telling how he caught Tajomaru, who is sitting, bound, beside him.

The scene itself, as described by the agent.

Tajomaru at the magistrate's, giving his own version of the story.

The scene itself, interrupted from time to time by returns to Tajomaru at the magistrate's. Tajomaru finds the couple in the forest, leads the man off with promise of treasure, attacks him. He then brings back the woman and shows her the husband bound. She tries to kill him but he overpowers her. He tries to rape her but finds that she submits to his intentions. Afterward, she insists that the men duel. Tajomaru wins, killing the husband.

Back at the gate, The priest tells the story he heard the wife tell the magistrate.

The wife at the magistrate's, telling her story.

The scene itself, interrupted by returns to the magistrate's office. Her story begins after the seduction. Her husband now

142

hates her. Distraught, she kills him, then tries to kill herself and fails.

At the gate, the three continue to talk, leading into the husband's story as told by the medium.

The medium at the magistrate's office. Speaking through her, the husband gives his version. The scene itself. His wife turns against him, tries to have him murdered. This fails but he kills himself. Later, after death, he feels someone remove the dagger.

At the gate, the woodcutter confesses that he knew more than he told.

His later version of the story. After the seduction the husband no longer respects his wife. She goads the two into fighting, a parody of the first fight scene described by the bandit himself. Again, however, he kills the husband. The wife flees, and Tajomaru is left alone.

At the gate, the three comment upon these various stories. The cry of an infant is heard. The commoner tries to take the baby's bedclothes, and the woodcutter in compassion takes the baby itself to give it a home. The priest says that his faith in man has been restored.

# Script Extract

Shot No.

255 *CU of the steps of the Rashomon with the rain pouring down. The dreary, loud sound of the rain. Visible above the steps are the three men, seated. The camera tilts up as the commoner stands; he comes forward, looks out at the sky, spits disgustedly, and turns back to the group.* (23 seconds

256 *MS. He rejoins the other two around the fire (pan).*

*Commoner:* I see. But the more I listen the more mixed up I get. (*He sits down.*) Women lead you on with their tears; they even fool themselves. Now if I believed what she said I'd really be mixed up.

*Priest:* But according to the husband's story . . .

*Commoner:* But he's dead. How could a dead man talk?

*Priest:* He spoke through a medium.

*Woodcutter:* Lies. (*He rises and comes toward the camera.*) His story was all lies.

*Priest:* Dead men tell no lies. (46 seconds

257 *CU of the commoner, in the foreground, and the priest.*

*Commoner:* All right, priest—why is that?

*Priest:* They must not. I must not believe that men are so sinful. (7 seconds

258 *CU of the two from reverse angle.*

*Commoner:* Oh, I don't object to that. After all, who's honest nowadays? Look, everyone wants to forget unpleasant things, so they

Shot No.

make up stories. It's easier that way. (*Grinning, he bites into a piece of fruit. The priest looks distraught.*) But never mind. Let's hear this dead man's story.                                                (*31 seconds*

259 *The ceiling and beams of the great gate illuminated by a tremendous flash of lightning.*                                                (*1 second*

260 *LS from above the three men as they look up. A roll of thunder is heard.*                                                                  (*3 seconds*

261 *MS of a fallen statue outside the gate. The rain falls even harder, flooding in rapid cascades past the statue.*          (*3 seconds*

262 *CU of the statue.*                                                (*2 seconds*

263 *CU of a hand bell being violently shaken in the air. The scene has abruptly shifted back to the prison courtyard.*          (*1 second*

264 *MS of the medium, a woman, her hair and robes blowing in the wind. She is rattling the bell, dancing madly. The bell clatters, the wind howls, and a weird, unearthly voice drones on like a record player slowing down. A drum beats slowly. The wind, voice, and drum continue through shot 273.*                          (*3 seconds*

265 *LS from above the medium. Behind her kneel the woodcutter and the priest. She circles the altar which has been placed in the courtyard, shaking the bell.*                                    (*6 seconds*

266 (=263) *CU of the bell being shaken.*                      (*1 second*

267 *MS of the medium writhing about on her feet. She begins to turn dizzily in circles. Suddenly she stops completely still.*

(*11 seconds*

268 *CU of the medium, now possessed by the other world.*

(*3 seconds*

269 *CU of the bell dropping from her hand.*                  (*1 second*

270 (=268) *CU. She turns abruptly to face the camera.*    (*1 second*

271 *LS. She rushes toward the foreground and stands, mouth open, her eyes wild, as the camera dollies in. Her mouth begins to move and suddenly the voice of the dead man is heard.*

*Samurai-Medium* (*as though at a great distance*): I am in darkness now. I am suffering in the darkness. Cursed be those who cast me into this hell of darkness. (*The medium starts to fall.*)    (*27 seconds*

Shot No.

272 *MS of the medium falling behind the altar to the ground. She moves convulsively on the ground, the camera panning with her.*

*(15 seconds*

273 *MS. She sits upright as the camera dollies in to an ECU. Her mouth opens and over the sound of the wind the voice of the samurai is heard.*

*Samurai-Medium:* The bandit, after attacking my wife, sat down beside her and tried to console her. (*The sound of the unearthly voice and drum stops abruptly.*)                    *(27 seconds*

274 *LS. The woods. In the clearing where the rape took place, the bandit is sitting beside the woman, talking to her, touching her arm to get her attention. The samurai's story is accompanied by a somber musical theme which plays over most of the scenes through shot 305.*

*Samurai-Medium (off):* She sat there on the leaves, looking down, looking at nothing. The bandit was cunning.

*Camera dollies back to reveal the husband bound in the foreground.*

*Samurai-Medium (off):* He told her that after she had given herself, she would no longer be able to live with her husband—why didn't she go with him, the bandit, rather than remain behind to be unhappy with her husband? He said he had only attacked her because of his great love for her.

*The husband turns his head toward them.*                    *(28 seconds*

275 *CU of the wife as she looks up as though she believes what Tajomaru is saying, her eyes dreamy.*

*Samurai-Medium (off):* My wife looked at him, her face soft, her eyes veiled.                    *(8 seconds*

276 *CU of the medium in the prison courtyard, as at the end of shot 273.*

*Samurai-Medium:* Never, in all of our life together, had I seen her more beautiful.                    *(6 seconds*

277 *CU of the husband in the woods; he stares at the others, then closes his eyes.*

*Samurai-Medium (off):* And what did my beautiful wife reply to the bandit in front of her helpless husband?                    *(17 seconds*

Shot No.

278 *MS. The woman looks up at Tajomaru, imploringly.*

*Woman:* Take me. Take me away with you.                    *(11 seconds*

279 *CU of the medium in the prison courtyard; she rises, the wind whipping her hair. The unearthly voice fades in and out.*

*Samurai-Medium:* That is what she said. (*The medium turns away, then abruptly faces the camera again.*) But that is not all she did, or else I would not now be in darkness.          *(15 seconds*

280 *MS, in the woods, from behind the husband's back. Tajomaru picks up the husband's sword and moves off screen. He returns, leading the woman off into the woods.*          *(10 seconds*

281 *CU of Tajomaru as he is jerked to a stop by the woman.*

*(2 seconds*

282 *MS of the woman holding Tajomaru by the hand. She points toward her husband.*

*Woman:* Kill him. As long as he is alive I cannot go with you. (*She moves behind Tajomaru, clutching him.*) Kill him!

*(12 seconds*

283 *MS of the medium in the prison courtyard, the wind howling about her.*

*Samurai-Medium:* I still hear those words. (*The medium writhes in circles on her knees.*) They are like a wind blowing me to the bottom of this dark pit. Has anyone ever uttered more pitiless words? Even the bandit was shocked to hear them.          *(25 seconds*

284 *ECU of the woman in the woods, clinging to the bandit's shoulder, digging her nails into him.*

*Woman:* Kill him!                                          *(7 seconds*

285 *LS from behind the husband's back; the woman takes a step toward the husband, pointing at him.*

*Woman:* Kill him—kill him!                                *(10 seconds*

286 *CU of Tajomaru, yanking the woman back to him. The look in his eyes makes her back off.*          *(8 seconds*

287 (=285) *LS. The bandit throws the woman from him.*

*(2 seconds*

Shot No.

288 *MS of the woman as she falls to the ground; the bandit places his foot on her back.* (*3 seconds*

289 *CU of the medium in the prison courtyard. She throws her head back and then forward and the dead man's laughter pours from her unmoving lips.* (*5 seconds*

290 (=285) *LS. Tajomaru, still standing over the woman, addresses the husband.*

*Tajomaru:* What do you want me to do with this woman? Kill her? Spare her? Just nod if you agree.

*The camera dollies around to show the husband in profile.*

*Samurai-Medium* (*off*): For these words I almost forgave the bandit. (*27 seconds*

291 *LS of the husband in the background; in the foreground (MS) Tajomaru continues pressing the woman to the ground with his foot.*

*Tajomaru:* What do you want me to do? Kill her? Let her go?

*Now Tajomaru walks toward the husband. As soon as he has gone a few steps, the woman springs up and runs away. Tajomaru turns to chase her, the camera panning to show them disappear among the trees. Her screams die away in the stillness of the woods.*

(*18 seconds*

292 *LS of the husband; still bound, he makes no effort to free himself.* (*9 seconds*

293 *MS of the husband.* (*6 seconds*

294 *CU of the husband.* (*4 seconds*

295 *Dead leaves on the ground in the late afternoon sun.*

*Samurai-Medium* (*off*): Hours later—I don't know how many.

(*5 seconds*

296 *MS of the husband's back. Tajomaru appears in the background, on the far side of the clearing, stomping along, slashing in disgust with some rope at the bushes. He walks up to the husband and stands looking down.* (*27 seconds*

297 *MS from reverse angle. Tajomaru takes his sword and cuts the captive's bonds.*

Shot No.

*Tajomaru:* Well, she got away. Now I'll have to worry about her talking. (*He turns and goes.*)
*The husband looks off after him, then up at the sky.*      *(45 seconds*

298  *Trees against the sky.*

*Samurai-Medium* (*off*): It was quiet.                    *(4 seconds*

299  *Dead leaves on the ground.*

*Samurai-Medium* (*off*): Then I heard someone crying . . .
*The camera tilts up along the leaves to reveal the husband (MS).*
*The bell-like tinkle of wind chimes is heard.*           *(11 seconds*

300  *CU of the husband crying. The camera dollies back and he rises to his feet. He moves painfully (pan), rests his head against a tree. There is the soft sound of grief, but it comes from the husband himself.*                                                  *(39 seconds*

301  *CU as he rests his head against the tree, sobbing. Finally he raises his head and begins to wander off, but stops when he notices something on the ground.*                            *(28 seconds*

302  *MS from behind the husband, the dagger sticking up before him. Slowly he goes to it, picks it up, and turns to walk back toward the camera, staring at the dagger.*                    *(32 seconds*

303  *LS as he moves into the clearing; he stops, raises the dagger high above his head and brutally thrusts it into his chest. He begins to fall.*                                              *(16 seconds*

304  *MS. His falling motion is completed by the medium in the prison courtyard (priest and woodcutter sit in the background). The medium sinks down as though dead, then slowly sits up.*

305  *CU of the medium.*

*Samurai-Medium:* Everything was quiet—how quiet it was. It grew dark and a mist seemed to envelop me. I lay quietly in this stillness. Then someone seemed to approach me. Softly, gently. Who could it have been? Then someone's hand grasped the dagger and drew it out. (*The medium falls forward.*)
*Music up and out.*                                         *(59 seconds*

306  *LS. In the shelter of the Rashomon, the priest and commoner*

Shot No.

*are seated at the fire; the woodcutter is pacing up and down, the
camera panning with him.*                                    *(18 seconds*

307 *MS as the woodcutter stops in the background and turns to the
others.*

*Woodcutter:* That's not true. There wasn't any dagger there—he
was killed by a sword.

*The commoner looks up from tending the fire. The woodcutter,
very agitated, moves farther into the background and sits down; the
commoner rises and goes back to sit beside him.*         *(40 seconds*

308 *MS from reverse angle. The commoner sits next to the woodcutter; the priest is in the background.*

*Commoner:* Now it's getting interesting. You must have seen the
whole thing. Why didn't you tell the police?

*Woodcutter:* I didn't want to get involved.

*Commoner:* But now you want to talk about it? Well, come on
and tell us then. Yours seems the most interesting of all these stories.
                                                              *(32 seconds*

309 *MS from reverse angle, the priest in the foreground.*

*Priest:* I don't want to hear. I don't want to have to listen to any
more horrible stories.

*The commoner stands and comes forward to the priest.*

*Commoner (to the priest)*: Stories like this are ordinary enough
now. I heard that demons used to live in the castle here by the gate,
but they all ran away, because what men do now horrified them so.
*(He goes back to the woodcutter.)*                          *(17 seconds*

# "Rashomon"
## by RYUNOSUKE AKUTAGAWA

It was a chilly evening. A samurai's servant stood under the Rashomon, waiting for a break in the rain.

No one else was under the wide gate. On the thick column, its crimson lacquer rubbed off here and there, perched a cricket. Since the Rashomon stands on Sujaku Avenue, a few other people at least, in sedge hat or nobleman's headgear, might have been expected to be waiting there for a break in the rainstorm. But no one was near except this man.

For the past few years the city of Kyoto had been visited by a series of calamities, earthquakes, whirlwinds, and fires, and Kyoto had been greatly devastated. Old chronicles say that broken pieces of Buddhist images and other Buddhist objects, with their lacquer, gold, or silver leaf worn off, were heaped up on roadsides to be sold as firewood. Such being the state of affairs in Kyoto, the repair of the Rashomon was out of the question. Taking advantage of the devastation, foxes and other wild animals made their dens in the ruins of the gate, and thieves and robbers found a home there too. Eventually it became customary to bring unclaimed corpses to this gate and abandon them. After dark it was so ghostly that no one dared approach.

Flocks of crows flew in from somewhere. During the daytime these cawing birds circled round the ridgepole of the gate. When

151

the sky overhead turned red in the afterlight of the departed sun, they looked like so many grains of sesame flung across the gate. But on that day not a crow was to be seen, perhaps because of the lateness of the hour. Here and there the stone steps, beginning to crumble, and with rank grass growing in their crevices, were dotted with the white droppings of crows. The servant, in a worn blue kimono, sat on the seventh and highest step, vacantly watching the rain. His attention was drawn to a large pimple irritating his right cheek.

As has been said, the servant was waiting for a break in the rain. But he had no particular idea of what to do after the rain stopped. Ordinarily, of course, he would have returned to his master's house, but he had been discharged just before. The prosperity of the city of Kyoto had been rapidly declining, and he had been dismissed by his master, whom he had served many years, because of the effects of this decline. Thus, confined by the rain, he was at a loss to know where to go. And the weather had not a little to do with his depressed mood. The rain seemed unlikely to stop. He was lost in thoughts of how to make his living tomorrow, helpless incoherent thoughts protesting an inexorable fate. Aimlessly he had been listening to the pattering of the rain on the Sujaku Avenue.

The rain, enveloping the Rashomon, gathered strength and came down with a pelting sound that could be heard far away. Looking up, he saw a fat black cloud impale itself on the tips of the tiles jutting out from the roof of the gate.

He had little choice of means, whether fair or foul, because of helpless circumstances. If he chose honest means, he would undoubtedly starve to death beside the wall or in the Sujaku gutter. He would be brought to this gate and thrown away like a stray dog. If he decided to steal. . . . His mind, after making the same detour time and again, came finally to the conclusion that he would be a thief.

But doubts returned many times. Though determined that he had no choice, he was still unable to muster enough courage to justify the conclusion that he must become a thief.

After a loud fit of sneezing he got up slowly. The evening chill of Kyoto made him long for the warmth of a brazier. The wind in the evening dusk howled through the columns of the gate. The cricket which had been perched on the crimson-lacquered column was already gone.

Ducking his neck, he looked around the gate as he drew up the shoulders of the blue kimono which he wore over his thin undergarments. He decided to spend the night there, if he could find a secluded corner sheltered from wind and rain. He found a broad lacquered stairway leading to the tower over the gate. No one would be there, except the dead, if there were any. So, taking care that the sword at his side did not slip out of the scabbard, he set foot on the lowest step of the stairs.

A few seconds later, halfway up the stairs, he saw a movement above. Holding his breath and huddling catlike in the middle of the broad stairs leading to the tower, he watched and waited. A light coming from the upper part of the tower shone faintly upon his right cheek. It was the cheek with the red, festering pimple visible under his stubby whiskers. He had expected only dead people inside the tower, but he had gone up only a few steps before he noticed a fire above, near which someone was moving. He saw a dull, yellow, flickering light which made the cobwebs hanging from the ceiling glow in a ghostly way. What sort of person would be making a fire in the Rashomon . . . and in a storm? The unknown, the evil terrified him.

Quietly as a lizard, the servant crept up to the top of the steep stairs. Crouching on all fours and stretching his neck as far as possible, he timidly peered into the tower.

As rumor had said, he found several corpses strewn carelessly about the floor. Since the glow of the light was feeble, he could not count the number. He could only see that some were naked and others clothed. Some were women, and all were sprawled on the floor with their mouths open or their arms outstretched, showing no more sign of life than so many clay dolls. One would doubt that they had ever been alive, so eternally silent were they. Their shoulders, breasts, and torsos stood out in the dim light; other parts vanished in shadow. The offensive smell of these decomposed corpses brought his hand to his nose.

The next moment his hand dropped and he stared. He caught sight of a ghoulish form bent over a corpse. It seemed to be an old woman, gaunt, gray-haired, and nunnish in appearance. With a pine torch in her right hand, she was gazing into the face of a corpse which had long black hair.

Seized more with horror than curiosity, he drew no breath for a time. He felt the hair of his head and body stand on end. As he watched, terrified, she wedged the torch between two floor boards and, laying hands on the head of the corpse, began to pull out the long hairs one by one, as a monkey kills the lice of her young. The hair came out smoothly with the movement of her hands.

As the hair came out, fear faded from his heart, and his hatred toward the old woman mounted. It grew beyond hatred, becoming a consuming antipathy against all evil. At this instant if anyone had brought up the question of whether he would starve to death or become a thief—the question which had occurred to him a little while ago—he would not have hesitated to choose death. His hatred of evil flared up like the piece of pine wood which the old woman had stuck in the floor.

He did not know why she pulled out the hair of the dead. Accordingly, he did not know whether her case was to be judged as good or bad. But in his eyes, pulling out the hair of the dead in the Rashomon on this story night was an unpardonable crime. Of course it never entered his mind that a little while ago he had thought of becoming a thief.

Then, summoning strength into his legs, he rose from the stairs and strode, hand on sword, right in front of the old creature. The head turned, terror in her eyes, and sprang up from the floor, trembling. For a moment she paused, poised there, then lunged for the stairs with a shriek.

"Wretch! Where are you going?" he shouted, barring the way of the trembling hag who tried to scurry past him. Still she attempted to claw her way by. He pushed her back to prevent her. . . . They struggled, fell among the corpses, and grappled there. The issue was never in doubt. In a moment he had her by the arm, twisted it, and forced her down to the floor. Her arms were nothing but skin and bones, and there was no more flesh on them than on the shanks of a chicken. No sooner was she on the floor than he drew his sword and thrust the silver-white blade before her very nose. She was silent. She trembled as if in a fit, and her eyes were open so wide that they were almost out of their sockets, and her breath came in hoarse gasps. The life of this wretch was his now. This thought cooled his boiling anger and brought a calm pride and satisfaction. He looked down at her, and said in a somewhat calmer voice:

"Look here, I'm not an officer of the High Police Commissioner. I'm a stranger who happened to pass by this gate. I won't bind you or do anything against you, but you must tell me what you're doing up here."

Then the old woman opened her eyes still wider, and gazed at his face intently with the sharp red eyes of a bird of prey. She moved her lips, which were wrinkled into her nose, as though she were chewing something. Her pointed Adam's apple moved in her thin throat. Then a panting sound like the cawing of a crow came from her throat:

"I pull the hair . . . I pull out the hair . . . to make a wig."

Her answer banished the unknown from their encounter and brought disappointment. Suddenly she was merely a trembling old woman there at his feet. A ghoul no longer: only a hag who makes wigs from the hair of the dead—to sell, for scraps of food. A cold contempt seized him. Fear left his heart, and his former hatred returned. These feelings must have been sensed by the other. The old creature, still clutching the hair she had pulled from the corpse, mumbled out these words in her harsh broken voice:

"Indeed, making wigs out of the hair of the dead may seem a great evil to you, but these that are here deserve no better. This woman, whose beautiful black hair I was pulling, used to sell dried snake flesh at the guard barracks, saying that it was dried fish. If she hadn't died of the plague, she'd be selling it now. The guards liked to buy from her, and used to say her fish was tasty. What she did couldn't be wrong, because if she hadn't, she would have starved to death. There was no other choice. If she knew I had to do this in order to live, she probably wouldn't care."

He sheathed his sword, and, with his left hand on its hilt, he listened to her meditatively. His right hand touched the big pimple on his cheek. As he listened, a certain courage was born in his heart —the courage he had not had when he sat under the gate a little while ago. A strange power was driving him in the opposite direction from the courage he had had when he seized the old woman. No longer did he wonder whether he should starve to death or become a thief. Starvation was so far from his mind that it was the last thing that would have entered it.

"Are you sure?" he asked in a mocking tone, when she finished talking. He took his right hand from his pimple, and, bending forward, seized her by the neck and said sharply:

"Then it's right if I rob you. I'd starve if I didn't."

He tore her clothes from her body and kicked her roughly down on the corpses as she struggled and tried to clutch his leg. Five steps, and he was at the top of the stairs. The yellow clothes he had wrested from her were under his arm, and in a twinkling he had rushed down the steep stairs into the abyss of night. The thunder of his descending steps pounded in the hollow tower, and then it was quiet.

# "In a Grove"
## by RYUNOSUKE AKUTAGAWA

THE TESTIMONY OF A WOODCUTTER QUESTIONED
BY A HIGH POLICE COMMISSIONER

Yes, sir. Certainly, it was I who found the body. This morning, as usual, I went to cut my daily quota of cedars, when I found the body in a grove in a hollow in the mountains.

The exact location? About 150 yards off the Yamashina stage road. It's an out-of-the-way grove of bamboo and cedars.

The body was lying flat on its back dressed in a bluish silk kimono and a wrinkled headdress of the Kyoto style. A single sword stroke had pierced the breast. The fallen bamboo blades around it were stained with bloody blossoms.

No, the blood was no longer flowing. The wound had dried up, I believe. And also, a gadfly was stuck fast there, hardly noticing my footsteps.

You ask me if I saw a sword or any such thing? No, nothing, sir. I found only a rope at the root of a cedar nearby. And . . . well, in addition to a rope, I found a comb. That was all. Apparently he must have made a battle of it before he was murdered, because the grass and fallen bamboo blades had been trampled down all around.

A horse was nearby? No, sir. It's hard enough for a man to enter, let alone a horse.

### The Testimony of a Traveling Buddhist Priest
### Questioned by a High Police Commissioner

The time? Certainly, it was about noon yesterday, sir. The unfortunate man was on the road from Sekiyama to Yamashina. He was
walking toward Sekiyama with a woman accompanying him on
horseback, who I have since learned was his wife. A scarf hanging
from her head hid her face from view. All I saw was the color of her
clothes, a lilac-colored suit. Her horse was a sorrel with a fine mane.
The lady's height? Oh, about four feet five inches. Since I am a
Buddhist priest, I took little notice about her details. Well, the man
was armed with a sword as well as a bow and arrows. And I remember that he carried some twenty-odd arrows in his quiver.

Little did I expect that he would meet such a fate. Truly, human
life is as evanescent as the morning dew or a flash of lightning. My
words are inadequate to express my sympathy for him.

### The Testimony of a Policeman Questioned
### by a High Police Commissioner

The man that I arrested? He is a notorious brigand called Tajomaru. When I arrested him, he had fallen off his horse. He was
groaning on the bridge at Awataguchi.

The time? It was in the early hours of last night. For the record, I
might say that the other day I tried to arrest him, but unfortunately
he escaped. He was wearing a dark-blue silk kimono and a large
plain sword. And, as you see, he got a bow and arrows somewhere.

You say that this bow and these arrows look like the ones owned
by the dead man? Then Tajomaru must be the murderer. The bow
wound with leather strips, the black lacquered quiver, the seventeen
arrows with hawk feathers—these were all in his possession, I believe.

Yes, sir, the horse is, as you say, a sorrel with a fine mane. A little
beyond the stone bridge I found the horse grazing by the roadside,

with his long rein dangling. Surely there is some providence in his having been thrown by the horse.

Of all the robbers prowling around Kyoto, this Tajomaru has brought the most grief to the women in town. Last autumn a wife who came to the mountain behind the Pindora of the Toribe Temple, presumably to pay a visit, was murdered, along with a girl. It has been suspected that it was his doing. If this criminal murdered the man, you cannot tell what he may have done with the man's wife. May it please your honor to look into this problem as well.

## The Testimony of an Old Woman Questioned by a High Police Commissioner

Yes, sir, that corpse is the man who married my daughter. He does not come from Kyoto. He was a samurai in the town of Kokufu in the province of Wakasa. His name was Kanazawa no Takehiro, and his age was twenty-six. He was of a gentle disposition, so I am sure he did nothing to provoke the anger of others.

My daughter? Her name is Masago, and her age is nineteen. She is a spirited, fun-loving girl, but I am sure she has never known any man except Takehiro. She has a small, oval, dark-complexioned face with a mole at the corner of her left eye.

Yesterday Takehiro left for Wakasa with my daughter. What a misfortune that things should have come to such a sad end! What has become of my daughter? I am resigned to giving up my son-in-law as lost, but the fate of my daughter worries me sick. For heaven's sake, leave no stone unturned to find her. I hate that robber Tajomaru, or whatever his name is. Not only my son-in-law, but my daughter. . . . (Her later words were drowned in tears.)

## Tajomaru's Confession

I killed him, but not her.

Where's she gone? I can't tell. Oh, wait a minute. No torture can make me confess what I don't know. Now things have come to such a head, I won't keep anything from you.

Yesterday a little past noon I met that couple. Just then a puff of wind blew, and raised her hanging scarf, so that I caught a glimpse of her face. Instantly it was again covered from my view. That may have been one reason; she looked like a Bodhisattva. At that moment I had made up my mind to capture her even if I had to kill her man.

Why? To me killing isn't a matter of such great consequence as you might think. When a woman is captured, her man has to be killed anyway. In killing, I use the sword I wear at my side. Am I the only one who kills people? You, you don't use your swords. You kill people with your power, with your money. Sometimes you kill them on the pretext of working for their good. It's true they don't bleed. They are in the best of health, but all the same you've killed them. It's hard to say who is a greater sinner, you or me. (An ironical smile.)

But it would be good if I could capture a woman without killing her man. So I made up my mind to capture her, and do my best not to kill him. But it's out of the question on the Yamashina stage road, so I managed to lure the couple into the mountains.

It was quite easy. I became their traveling companion, and I told them there was an old mound in the mountain over there, and that I had dug it open and found many mirrors and swords. I went on to tell them I'd buried the things in a grove behind the mountain, and that I'd like to sell them at a low price to anyone who would care to have them. Then . . . you see, isn't greed terrible? He was beginning to be moved by my talk before he knew it. In less than half an hour they were driving their horse toward the mountain with me.

When he reached the grove, I told them that the treasures were buried in it, and I asked them to come and see. The man had no objection—he was blinded by greed. The woman said she would wait on horseback. It was natural for her to say so, at the sight of a thick grove. To tell you the truth, my plan worked just as I wished. So I went into the grove with him, leaving her behind alone.

The grove is only bamboo for some distance. About fifty yards ahead there's a rather open clump of cedars. It was a convenient spot for my purpose. Pushing my way through the grove, I told him a plausible lie that the treasures were buried under the cedars. When I told him this, he laboriously pushed his way toward the slender cedars visible through the grove. After a while the bamboo thinned out, and we came to where a number of cedars grew in a row. As soon as we got there, I seized him from behind. Because he was a trained, sword-bearing warrior, he was quite strong, but he was taken by surprise, so there was no help for him. I soon tied him up to the root of a cedar.

Where did I get a rope? Thank heaven, being a robber, I had rope with me, since I might have to scale a wall at any moment. Of course it was easy to stop him from calling out by gagging his mouth with fallen bamboo leaves.

When I disposed of him, I went to his woman and asked her to come and see him, because he seemed to have been suddenly taken sick. It's needless to say that this plan also worked well. The woman, her sedge hat off, came into the depths of the grove, where I led her by the hand. The instant she caught sight of her husband, she drew a small sword. I've never seen a woman of such violent temper. If I'd been off guard, I'd have got a thrust in my side. I dodged, but she kept on slashing at me. She might have wounded me deeply or killed me. But I'm Tajomaru. I managed to strike down her small sword without drawing my own. The most spirited woman is defenseless without a weapon. At last I could satisfy my desire for her without taking her husband's life.

Yes . . . without taking his life. I didn't want to kill him. I was about to run away from the grove, leaving the woman behind in tears, when she frantically clung to my arm. In broken fragments of words, she asked that either her husband or I die. She said it was more trying than death to have her shame known to two men. She gasped out that she wanted to be the wife of whichever survived. Then a furious desire to kill him seized me.

Telling you in this way, no doubt I seem a crueler man than you. But that's because you didn't see her face. Especially her burning eyes at that moment. As I saw her eye to eye, I wanted to make her my wife even if I were to be struck by lightning. I wanted to make her my wife . . . this single desire filled my mind. This was not simply lust, as you might think. At that time if I'd had no other desire than lust, I surely wouldn't have minded knocking her down and running away. Then I wouldn't have stained my sword with his blood. But the moment I gazed at her face in the dark grove, I decided not to leave without killing him.

But I didn't like to resort to unfair means to kill him. I untied him and told him to cross swords with me. The rope that was found at the root of the cedar is the rope I dropped at the time. Furious with anger, he drew his thick sword. And quick as a wink, he sprang at me ferociously, without speaking a word. I needn't tell you how our fight turned out. The twenty-third stroke . . . please remember this. I'm impressed with this fact still. Nobody under the sun has ever clashed swords with me twenty strokes. (A cheerful smile.)

When he fell, I turned toward her, lowering my blood-stained sword. But to my great astonishment she was gone. I wondered where she had run to. I looked for her in the clump of cedars. I listened, but heard only a groaning sound from the throat of the dying man.

As soon as we crossed swords, she may have run away through the grove to call for help. When I thought of that, I decided it was a matter of life and death to me. So, robbing him of his sword, and bow and arrows, I ran out to the mountain road. There I found her horse still grazing quietly. It would be a waste of words to tell you the later details, but before I entered town I had already parted with the sword. That's my confession. I know that my head will be hung in chains anyway, so give me the maximum penalty. (A defiant attitude.)

THE CONFESSION OF A WOMAN WHO HAS
COME TO THE SHIMIZU TEMPLE

That man in the blue silk kimono, after forcing me to yield to him, laughed mockingly as he looked at my bound husband. How horrified my husband must have been! But no matter how hard he he struggled in agony, the rope cut into him all the more tightly. In spite of myself I ran stumblingly toward his side. Or rather I tried to run toward him, but the man knocked me down. Just at that moment I saw an indescribable light in my husband's eyes. Something beyond expression . . . his eyes make me shudder even now. That instantaneous look of my husband, who couldn't speak a word, told me all his heart. The flash in his eyes was neither anger nor sorrow . . . only a cold light, a look of loathing. More struck by the look in his eyes than by the blow of the thief, I called out in spite of myself and fell unconscious.

In the course of time I came to, and found that the man in blue silk was gone. I saw only my husband still bound to the root of the cedar. I raised myself from the bamboo blades with difficulty, and looked into his face; but the expression in his eyes was just the same as before.

Beneath the cold contempt in his eyes, there was hatred. Shame, grief, and anger . . . I don't know how to express my heart at that time. Reeling to my feet, I went up to my husband.

"Takehiro," I said to him, "since things have come to this pass, I cannot live with you. I'm determined to die . . . but you must die, too. You saw my shame. I can't leave you alive as you are."

This was all I could say. Still he went on gazing at me with loathing and contempt. My heart breaking, I looked for his sword. It must have been taken by the robber. Neither his sword nor his bow and arrow were to be seen in the grove. But fortunately my small sword was lying at my feet. Raising it overhead, once more I said, "Now give me your life. I'll follow you right away."

When he heard these words, he moved his lips with difficulty. Since his mouth was stuffed with leaves, of course his voice could not be heard. But at a glance I understood his words. Despising me, his look said only, "Kill me." Neither conscious nor unconscious, I stabbed the small sword through the lilac-colored kimono into his breast.

Again at this time I must have fainted. By the time I managed to look up, he had already breathed his last—still in bonds. A streak of sinking sunlight streamed through the clump of cedars and bamboos, and shone on his pale face. Gulping down my sobs, I untied the rope from his dead body. And . . . and what has become of me since, I have no more strength to tell you. Anyway, I hadn't the strength to die. I stabbed my own throat with the small sword, I threw myself into a pond at the foot of the mountain, and I tried to kill myself in many ways. Unable to end my life, I am still living in

dishonor. (A lonely smile.) Worthless as I am, I must have been for-
saken even by the most merciful Kwannon. I killed my own husband. I was violated by the robber. Whatever can I do? Whatever
can I . . . I . . . (Gradually, violent sobbing.)


### THE STORY OF THE MURDERED MAN, AS TOLD THROUGH A MEDIUM

After violating my wife, the robber, sitting there, began to speak
comforting words to her. Of course I couldn't speak. My whole
body was tied fast to the root of a cedar. But meanwhile I winked
at her many times, as much as to say, "Don't believe the robber."
I wanted to convey some such meaning to her. But my wife, sitting
dejectedly on the bamboo leaves, was staring at her lap. To all
appearances, she was listening to his words. I was racked with jealousy. In the meantime the robber went on with his clever talk,
from one subject to another. The robber finally made his brazen
proposal. "Once your virtue is stained, you won't get along well
with your husband, so won't you be my wife instead? It's my love
for you that made me violent toward you."

While the criminal talked, my wife raised her face as if in a
trance. She had never looked so beautiful as at that moment. What
did my beautiful wife say in answer to him while I was sitting
bound there? I am lost in space, but I have never thought of her
answer without burning with anger and jealousy. Truly she said,
"Then take me away with you wherever you go."

This is not the whole of her sin. If that were all, I would not be
tormented so much in the dark. When she was leaving the grove as
if in a dream, her hand in the robber's, she suddenly turned pale,
and pointed at me tied to the root of the cedar, and said, "Kill him!
I cannot marry you as long as he lives." "Kill him!" she cried many
times, as if she had gone crazy. Even now these words threaten to
blow me headlong into the bottomless abyss of darkness. Has such
a hateful thing come out of a human mouth ever before? Have such
cursed words ever struck a human ear, even once? Even once such
a . . . (A sudden cry of scorn.) At these words the robber himself

turned pale. "Kill him!" she cried, clinging to his arms. Looking hard at her, he answered neither yes nor no. . . . But hardly had I thought about his answer before she had been knocked down into the bamboo leaves. (Again a cry of scorn.) Quietly folding his arms, he looked at me and said, "What would you like done with her? Kill her or save her? You have only to nod. Kill her?" For these words alone I would like to pardon his crime.

While I hesitated, she shrieked and ran into the depths of the grove. The robber instantly snatched at her, but he failed even to grasp her sleeve.

After she ran away, he took up my sword, and my bow and arrows. With a single stroke he cut one of my bonds. I remember his mumbling, "My fate is next." Then he disappeared from the grove. All was silent after that. No, I heard someone crying. Untying the rest of my bonds, I listened carefully, and noticed that it was my own crying. (Long silence.)

I raised my exhausted body from the root of the cedar. In front of me there was shining the small sword which my wife had dropped. I took it up and stabbed it into my breast. A bloody lump rose to my mouth, but I felt no pain. When my breast grew cold, everything was as silent as the dead in their graves. What profound silence! Not a single bird note was heard in the sky over this grave in the hollow of the mountains. Only a lonely light lingered on the cedars and the mountain. The light gradually grew fainter, till the cedars and bamboo were lost to view. Lying there, I was enveloped in deep silence.

Then someone crept up to me. I tried to see who it was. But darkness had already been gathering round me. Someone . . . that someone drew the small sword softly out of my breast in its invisible hand. At the same time blood again flowed into my mouth. And once and for all I sank down into the darkness of space.

# Filmography

The release dates given in this filmography refer to the opening date of the initial release in Japan. The commonly used English title of each film is followed by the Japanese title and then, in order, alternative English titles, French titles, German titles. In preparing this filmography I am particularly indebted to the assistance of UniJapan Film.

1. *Sanshiro Sugata (Sugata Sanshiro)*, March 25, 1943

*(Judo Saga; La légende de judo—I; Sanshiro Sugata)*
2,166 meters; 80 minutes. Reconstructed and re-released, 1952; reconstructed negative in existence; prints in general circulation. A Toho Production. U.S. rights held by J. Walter Reade, Assoc.
Produced by Keiji Matsuzaki. Scenario by Akira Kurosawa. After the novel by Tsuneo Tomita. Photographed by Akira Mimura. Art Direction by Masao Totsuka. Music by Seichi Suzuki. Edited by Toshio Goto and Akira Kurosawa.
With Susumu Fujita, Denjiro Okoohi, Takashi Shimura, Yukiko Todoroki, Yoshio Kosugi, Ranko Hanai, Ryunosuke Tsukigata, Akitake Kono, Soshi Kiyokawa, Kunio Mita, Akira Nakamura, Sugisaku Aoyama, Kuninori Kodo, Ichiro Sugai.

2. *The Most Beautiful (Ichiban Utsukushiku)*, April 13, 1944

*(Most Beautifully; Le plus doux; Le plus beau; Am allerschönsten)*
2,324 meters; 85 minutes. Original negative in existence; no prints in general circulation. A Toho Production. No U.S. distribution.

Produced by Motohiko Ito. Scenario by Akira Kurosawa. Photographed by Joji Ohara. Art Direction by Teruaki Abe. Music by Seichi Suzuki.

With Takashi Shimura, Ichiro Sugai, Yoko Yaguchi, Koyuri Tanima, Takako Irie, Toshiko Hattori.

3. *Sanshiro Sugata—Part Two* (*Zoku Sugata Sanshiro*), May 3, 1945

(*Judo Saga—II; La légende de judo—II; Sugata Sanshiro Fortsetzung*)

2,268 meters; 83 minutes. No original negative, no dupe-neg; no prints in circulation. A Toho Production. No U.S. distribution.

Produced by Motohiko Ito. Scenario by Akira Kurosawa. After the novel by Tsuneo Tomita. Photographed by Hiroshi Suzuki. Art Direction by Kazuo Kubo. Music by Seichi Suzuki.

With Susumu Fujita, Denjiro Okochi, Akitake Kono, Ryunosuke Tsukigata, Yukiko Todoroki, Soshi Kiyokawa.

4. *They Who Step on the Tiger's Tail* (*Tora no O o Fumu Otokotachi*), August 1945

(*The Men Who Tread on the Tiger's Tail; Walkers on the Tiger's Tail; They Who Step on the Tail of the Tiger; Sur la queue du tigre; Les hommes qui marchèrent sur la queue du tigre; Die Männer, die dem Tiger auf den Schwanz traten; Die Tigerfährte*)

1,575 meters; 58 minutes. Released: 24 April, 1952. Original negative in existence; prints in circulation. A Toho Production. U.S. distribution: Audio/Brandon Films.

Produced by Motohiko Ito. Scenario by Akira Kurosawa. After the Kabuki *Kanjincho*. Photographed by Takeo Ito. Art Direction by Kazuo Kubo. Music by Tadashi Hattori.

With Denjiro Okochi, Susumu Fujita, Masayuki Mori, Takashi Shimura, Aritake Kono, Yoshio Kosugi, Dekao Yoko, Hanshiro Iwai, Kenichi Enomoto.

5. *Those Who Make Tomorrow* (*Asu o Tsukuru Hitobito*), May 2, 1946

*(Ceux qui font l'avenir; Ceux qui bâtissent l'avenir; Erbauer des Morgens)*

2,250 meters; 81 minutes. Original negative in existence; no prints in existence. A Toho Production. No U.S. distribution.

Produced by Ryo Takei, Sojiro Motoki, Keiji Matsuzaki, and Tomoyuki Tanaka. Scenario by Yusaku Yamagata and Kajiro Yamamoto. Photographed by Takeo Ito, Mitsui Miura, and Taiichi Kankura. Directed by Kajiro Yamamoto, Hideo Sekigawa, and Akira Kurosawa.

With Kenji Susukida, Chieko Takehisa, Chieko Nakakita, Mitsue Tachibana, Masayuki Mori, Sumie Tsubaki, Ichiro Chiba, Hyo Kitazawa, Itoko Kono, Takashi Shimura, Masao Shimizu, Yuriko Hamada, Sayuri Tanima.

6. *No Regrets for Our Youth (Waga Seishun ni Kuinashi)*, October 29, 1946

*(No Regrets for My Youth; Je ne regrette rien de ma jeunesse; Je ne regrette pas ma jeunesse; Kein Bedauern für meine Jugend)*

3,024 meters; 110 minutes. Original negative in existence; no prints in circulation. A Toho Production. No U.S. distribution.

Produced by Keiji Matsuzaki. Scenario by Eijiro Hisaita and Akira Kurosawa. Photographed by Asakazu Nakai. Art Direction by Keiji Kitagawa. Music by Tadashi Hattori.

With Denjiro Okochi, Eiko Miyoshi, Setsuko Hara, Susumu Fujita, Kuninori Kodo, Haruko Sugimura, Aritake Kono, Takashi Shimura.

7. *One Wonderful Sunday (Subarashiki Nichiyobi)*, June 25, 1947

*(Wonderful Sunday; Un merveilleux dimanche; Ein wunderschöner Sonntag)*

2,950 meters; 108 minutes. Original negative in existence; no prints in circulation. A Toho Production. No U.S. distribution.

Produced by Sojiro Motogi. Scenario by Keinosuke Uegusa and Akira Kurosawa. Photographed by Asakazu Nakai. Art Direction by Kazuo Kubo. Music by Tadashi Hattori.

With Isao Numasaki, Chieko Nakakita, Ichiro Sugai, Midori Ari-
yama, Masao Shimizu.

8. *Drunken Angel (Yoidore Tenshi)*, April 27, 1948

*(A Drunken Angel; L'Ange ivre; Der trunkene Engel)*
2,690 meters; 98 minutes. Original unreleased version: 4,105 meters;
150 minutes. Original negative of cut version in existence; no prints
of uncut version in existence; cut prints in general circulation. A
Toho Production. U.S. distribution: Audio/Brandon Films.

Produced by Sojiro Motoki. Scenario by Keinosuke Uegusa and
Akira Kurosawa. Photographed by Takeo Ito. Art Direction by So
Matsuyama. Lighting by Kinzo Yoshizawa. Music by Fumio Haya-
saka.

With Takashi Shimura, Toshiro Mifune, Reisaburo Yamamoto,
Chieko Nakakita, Michiyo Kogure, Noriko Sengoku, Eitaro Shindo,
Choko Iida.

9. *The Quiet Duel (Shizukanaru Ketto)*, March 13, 1949

*(A Silent Duel; Le duel silencieux; Das stumme Duel)*
2,591 meters; 95 minutes. Original negative in existence; prints
available upon application. A Daiei Production. No U.S. distribution.

Produced by Sojiro Motogi and Hisao Ichikawa. Scenario by Sen-
kichi Taniguchi and Akira Kurosawa. After a play by Kazuo Kikuta.
Photographed by Shoichi Aisaka. Art Direction by Koichi Imai.
Music by Akira Ifukube.

With Toshiro Mifune, Takashi Shimura, Miki Sanjo, Kenjiro Ue-
mura, Chieko Nakakita, Noriko Sengoku.

10. *Stray Dog (Nora Inu)*, October 17, 1949

*(Le chien enragé; Ein herrenloser Hund)*
3,342 meters; 122 minutes. Original negative in existence; prints in
general circulation. A Shintoho Production; acquired by Toho in
1959. U.S. distribution: Audio/Brandon Films.

Produced by Sojiro Motogi. Scenario by Ryuzo Kikushima and Akira Kurosawa. Photographed by Asakazu Nakai. Art Direction by So Matsuyama. Music by Fumio Hayasaka.

With Toshiro Mifune, Takashi Shimura, Ko Kimura, Keiko Awaji, Reisaburo Yamamoto, Noriko Sengoku.

## 11. *Scandal* (*Shubun*), April 30, 1950

*(Scandale; Skandal)*

2,860 meters; 104 minutes. Original negative in existence. A Sho-chiku Production. U.S. distribution: Shochiku 16.

Produced by Takashi Koide. Scenario by Ryuzo Kikushima and Akira Kurosawa. Photographed by Toshio Ubukata. Art Direction by Tatsuo Hamada. Music by Fumio Hayasaka.

With Toshiro Mifune, Yoshiko Yamaguchi, Takashi Shimura, Yoko Katsuragi, Noriko Sengoku, Eitaro Ozawa, Bokuzen Hidari, Kuni-nori Kodo.

## 12. *Rashomon* (*Rashomon*), August 25, 1950

*(Rashomon; Rashomon)*

2,406 meters; 88 minutes. Original negative in existence; dupe-negs in existence, also a number of 16-mm. dupe-negs; prints in general circulation. A Daiei Production. U.S. distribution: Janus Films, Inc.

Produced by Jingo Minoru (later titles: Produced by Masaichi Nagata). Scenario by Shinobu Hashimoto and Akira Kurosawa. After two stories by Ryunosuke Akutagawa. Photographed by Kazuo Miyagawa. Art Direction by So Matsuyama. Music by Fumio Haya-saka.

With Toshiro Mifune, Masayuki Mori, Machiko Kyo, Takashi Shimura, Minoru Chiaki, Kichijiro Ueda, Daisuke Kato, Fumiko Homma.

## 13. *The Idiot* (*Hakuchi*), May 23, 1951

*(L'Idiot; Der Idiot)*

Original unreleased version: 265 minutes. Released version: 166 minutes. Cut negative also in existence. A Shochiku Production. U.S. distribution (166 min. version): New Yorker Films, Inc.

Produced by Takashi Koide. Scenario by Eijiro Hisaita and Akira Kurosawa. After the novel of Dostoevsky. Photographed by Toshio Ubukata. Art Direction by So Matsuyama. Music by Fumio Hayasaka.

With Masayuki Mori, Toshiro Mifune, Setsuko Hara, Takashi Shimura, Yoshiko Kuga.

14. *Ikiru* (*Living*), October 9, 1952

(*To Live; Doomed; Vivre; Vivre enfin un seul jour; Leben!*)

3,918 meters; 143 minutes. Original negative destroyed; several dupe-negs in existence; prints in general circulation. A Toho Production. U.S. distribution: Audio/Brandon Films.

Produced by Shojiro Motoki. Scenario by Shinobu Hashimoto, Hideo Oguni, and Akira Kurosawa. Photographed by Asakazu Nakai. Art Direction by So Matsuyama. Lighting by Shigeru Mori. Sound Recording by Fumio Yanoguchi. Music by Fumio Hayasaka.

With Takashi Shimura, Nobuo Kaneko, Kyoko Seki, Makoto Kobori, Kumeko Urabe, Yoshie Minami, Miki Odagiri, Kamatari Fujiwara, Minosuke Yamada, Haruo Tanaka, Bokuzen Hidari, Shinichi Himori, Nobuo Nakamura, Kazuo Abe, Masao Shimizu, Ko Kimura, Atsushi Watanabe, Yunosuke Ito, Yatsuko Tanami, Fuyuki Murakami, Seiji Miyaguchi, Daisuke Kato, Kin Sugai, Eiko Miyoshi, Fumiko Homma, Ichiro Chiba.

15. *Seven Samurai* (*Shichinin no Samurai*), April 26, 1954

(*The Magnificent Seven; Les sept samouraïs; Die sieben Samurai*)

Original released version: 200 minutes. Original negative reconstructed (1970): prints upon application. Secondary release version: 160 min.; prints upon application. U.S. release version (1): 141 minutes. U.S. distribution: Audio/Brandon Films. U.S. release version (2), ca. 90 min., dubbed: Estate of RKO Films. A Toho Production.

Produced by Shojiro Motoki. Scenario by Shinobu Hashimoto, Hideo Oguni, and Akira Kurosawa. Photographed by Asakazu Nakai. Lighting by Shigero Mori. Art Direction by So Matsuyama. Art Consultation by Seison Maeda and Kohei Ezaki. Fencing Direction by Yoshio Sugino. Archery Direction by Ienori Kaneko and Shigeru Endo. Sound Recording by Fumio Yanoguchi. Music by Fumio Hayasaka. Assistant Director—Hiromichi Horikawa.

With Takashi Shimura, Toshiro Mifune, Yoshio Inaba, Seiji Miyaguchi, Minoru Chiaki, Daisuke Kato, Ko Kimura, Kamatari Fujiwara, Kuninori Kodo, Bokuzen Hidari, Yoshio Kosugi, Yoshio Tsuchiya, Keiji Sakakida, Jiro Kumagai, Haruko Toyama, Tsuneo Katagiri, Yasuhisa Tsutsumi, Keiko Tsushima, Toranosuke Ogawa, Yu Akitsu, Noriko Sengoku, Gen Shimizu, Jun Tatari, Atsushi Watanabe, Sojin Kamiyama, Kichijiro Ueda, Shimpei Takagi, Akira Tani, Haruo Nakajima, Takashi Narita, Senkichi Omura, Shuno Takahara, Masanobu Okubo.

16. *Record of a Living Being* (*Ikimono no Kiroku*), November 22, 1955

(*I Live in Fear; What the Birds Knew; Chronique d'un être vivant; Vivre dans la peur; Notes d'un être vivant; Si les oiseaux savaient; Bilanz eines Lebens; Ein Leben in Angst*)

3,103 meters; 113 minutes. Export version: 2,838 meters; 104 minutes. Original negative extant. A Toho Production. U.S. distribution: Audio/Brandon Films.

Produced by Shojiro Motoki. Scenario by Shinobu Hashimoto, Hideo Oguni, and Akira Kurosawa. Photographed by Asakazu Nakai. Lighting by Kuichiro Kishida. Art Direction by Yoshiro Muraki. Sound Recording by Fumio Yanoguchi. Music by Fumio Hayasaka—completed by Masaru Sato.

With Toshiro Mifune, Eiko Miyoshi, Yutaka Sada, Minoru Chiaki, Haruko Togo, Kyoko Aoyama, Kiyomi Mizunoya, Saoko Yonemura, Akemi Negishi, Kichijiro Ueda, Masao Shimizu, Noriko Sengoku, Yoichi Tachikawa, Takashi Shimura, Kazuo Kato, Eijiro Tono, Ken Mitsuda, Toranosuke Ogawa, Kamatari Fujiwara, Nobuo Nakamura.

17. *The Throne of Blood* (*Kumonosu-jo*), January 15, 1957

(*The Castle of the Spider's Web; Cobweb Castle; Kumonosu-Djo, Le chateau de l'araignée; Le trône sanglant; Macbeth; Das Schloss im Spinnennetz*)

3,006 meters; 110 minutes. Original negative in existence; prints in general circulation. A Toho Production. U.S. distribution: Audio/ Brandon Films.

Produced by Shojiro Motoki and Akira Kurosawa. Scenario by Shinobu Hashimoto, Ryuzo Kikushima, Hideo Oguni, and Akira Kurosawa. After Shakespeare's *Macbeth*. Photographed by Asakazu Nakai. Art Direction by Yoshiro Muraki and Kohei Ezaki. Sound Recording by Fumio Yanoguchi. Music by Masaru Sato.

With Toshiro Mifune, Isuzu Yamada, Minoru Chiaki, Akira Kubo, Takamaru Sasaki, Yoichi Tachikawa, Takashi Shimura, Chieko Naniwa.

18. *The Lower Depths* (*Donzoko*), September 17, 1957

(*Les bas-fonds; Nachtasyl*)

3,744 meters; 137 minutes. Original negative in existence; prints in general circulation. A Toho Production. U.S. distribution: Audio/ Brandon Films.

Produced by Shojiro Motoki and Akira Kurosawa. Scenario by Hideo Oguni and Akira Kurosawa. Based on Gorky's play. Photographed by Kazuo Yamasaki. Art Direction by Yoshiro Muraki. Music by Masaru Sato.

With Toshiro Mifune, Isuzu Yamada, Ganjiro Nakamura, Kyoko Kagawa, Bokuzen Hidari, Minoru Chiaki, Kamatari Fujiwara, Eijiro Tono, Eiko Miyoshi, Akemi Negishi, Koji Mitsui, Nijiko Kiyokawa, Haruo Tanaka, Kichijiro Ueda.

19. *The Hidden Fortress* (*Kakushi Toride no San-Akunin*), December 28, 1958

(*Three Bad Men in a Hidden Fortress; Trois salauds dans une forteresse cachée; La forteresse cachée; Die verborgene Festung*)

Original version: 3,802 meters; 139 minutes. Export version: 3,453 meters; 126 minutes. Original negative extant; prints in general circulation. A Toho Production. U.S. Distribution: Film Images/ Radim Films.

Produced by Masumi Fujimoto and Akira Kurosawa. Scenario by Shinobu Hashimoto, Ryuzo Kikushima, Hideo Oguni, and Akira Kurosawa. Photographed by Kazuo Yamasaki (widescreen). Lighting by Ichiro Inohara. Art Direction by Yoshiro Muraki and Kohei Ezaki. Sound Recording by Fumio Yanoguchi. Music by Masaru Sato.

With Toshiro Mifune, Misa Uehara, Takashi Shimura, Susumu Fujita, Eiko Miyoshi, Minoru Chiaki, Kamatari Fujiwara, Toshiko Higuchi, Kichijiro Ueda, Koji Mitsui.

20. *The Bad Sleep Well* (*Warui Yatsu Hodo Yoku Nemuru*), September 4, 1960

(*The Worse You Are the Better You Sleep; The Rose in the Mud; Les salauds dorment en paix; Les salauds se portent bien; Die Verworfenen schlafen gut; Die Bösen schlafen gut*)

Original version: 4,123 meters; 151 minutes. Export version: 3,700 meters; 135 minutes. Original negative extant; prints in general circulation. A Kurosawa Films Production. Distributed by Toho. U.S. distribution: Audio/Brandon Films.

Produced by Tomoyuki Tanaka and Akira Kurosawa. Scenario by Shinobu Hashimoto, Hideo Oguni, Ryuzo Kikushima, Eijiro Hisaita, and Akira Kurosawa. Photographed by Yuzuru Aizawa (widescreen). Art Direction by Yoshiro Muraki. Lighting by Ichiro Inohara. Sound Recording by Fumio Yanoguchi and Hisashi Shimogawa. Music by Masaru Sato.

With Toshiro Mifune, Takeshi Kato, Masayuki Mori, Takashi Shimura, Akira Nishimura, Kamatari Fujiwara, Gen Shimizu, Kyoko Kagawa, Tatsuya Mihashi, Kyu Sazanka, Chishu Ryu, Seiji Miyaguchi, Nobuo Nakamura, Susumu Fujita, Koji Mitsui.

21. *Yojimbo* (*Yojimbo*), April 25, 1961
(*The Bodyguard; Le garde du corps; Die Leibwache*)

3,025 meters; 110 minutes. Original negative in existence; prints in general circulation. A Kurosawa Films Production. Distributed by Toho. U.S. distribution: Audio/Brandon Films and Janus Films, Inc.

Produced by Tomoyuki Tanaka and Ryuzo Kikushima. Scenario by Ryuzo Kikushima and Akira Kurosawa. Photographed by Kazuo Miyagawa (widescreen). Art Direction by Yoshiro Muraki. Lighting by Choshiro Ishii. Sound Recording by Hisashi Shimonaga and Choshichiro Mikami. Music by Masaru Sato.

With Toshiro Mifune, Eijiro Tono, Kamatari Fujiwara, Takashi Shimura, Seizaburo Kawazu, Isuzu Yamada, Hiroshi Tachikawa, Kyu Sazanka, Tatsuya Nakadai, Daisuke Kato, Ikio Sawamura, Akira Nishimura, Yoshio Tsuchiya, Yoko Tsukasa, Susumu Fujita.

## 22. Sanjuro (Tsubaki Sanjuro), January 1, 1962

*(Sanjuro; Sanjuro)*

2,685 meters; 96 minutes. Original negative in existence; prints in general circulation. A Kurosawa Film Production. Distributed by Toho. No U.S. distribution.

Produced by Tomoyuki Tanaka and Ryuzo Kikushima. Scenario by Ryuzo Kikushima, Hideo Oguni, and Akira Kurosawa. After the novel by Shugoro Yamamoto. Photographed by Fukuzo Koizumi (widescreen). Art Direction by Yoshiro Muraki. Lighting by Ichiro Inohara. Sound Recording by Wataru Konuma and Hisashi Shimonaga. Music by Masaru Sato. Advisor on Swordplay—Ryu Kuze.

With Toshiro Mifune, Tatsuya Nakadai, Yuzo Kayama, Akihiko Hirata, Kunie Tanaka, Hiroshi Tachikawa, Tatsuhiko Hari, Tatsuyoshi Ehara, Kenzo Matsui, Yoshio Tsuchiya, Akira Kubo, Takashi Shimura, Kamatari Fujiwara, Masao Shimizu, Yunosuke Ito, Takako Irie, Reiko Dan, Keiju Kobayashi.

## 23. High and Low (Tengoku to Jigoku), March 1, 1963

*(Heaven and Hell; The Ransom; Le paradis et l'enfer; Entre le ciel et l'enfer; Zwischen Himmel und Hölle)*

3,924 meters; 143 minutes. Original negative in existence; prints in general circulation. A Kurosawa Films Production. Distributed by Toho. U.S. distribution: J. Walter Reade, Assoc.

Produced by Tomoyuki Tanaka and Ryuzo Kikushima. Scenario by Ryuzo Kikushima, Hideo Oguni, and Akira Kurosawa. After the novel *King's Ransom* by Ed McBain (Evan Hunter). Photographed by Asakazu Nakai (widescreen). Art Direction by Yoshiro Muraki. Lighting by Ichiro Inohara. Sound Recording by Hisahi Shimonaga. Music by Masaru Sato.

With Toshiro Mifune, Kyoko Kagawa, Tatsuya Mihashi, Yutaka Sada, Tatsuya Nakadai, Takashi Shimura, Susumu Fujita, Kenjiro Ishiyama, Ko Kimura, Takeshi Kato, Yoshio Tsuchiyama, Hiroshi Unayama, Koji Mitsui, Tsutomu Yamazaki.

### 24. Red Beard (*Akahige*), April 3, 1965

(*Barbe rouge; Rotbart*)

5,069 meters; 185 minutes. Original negative in existence; prints in general circulation. A Kurosawa Films Production. Distributed by Toho. U.S. distribution: Audio/Brandon Films.

Produced by Ryuzo Kikushima and Tomoyuki Tanaka. Scenario by Ryuzo Kikushima, Hideo Oguni, Masato Ide, and Akira Kurosawa. After the novel by Shugoro Yamamoto. Photographed by Asakazu Nakai and Takao Saito (widescreen). Art Direction by Yoshiro Muraki. Lighting by Hiromitsu Mori. Sound Recording by Shin Watarai (four-track). Music by Masaru Sato.

With Toshiro Mifune, Yuzo Kayama, Yoshio Tsuchiya, Tatsuyoshi Ehara, Reiko Dan, Kyoko Kagawa, Kamatari Fujiwara, Akemi Negishi, Tsutomu Yamazaki, Miyuki Kuwano, Eijiro Tono, Takashi Shimura, Terumi Niki, Haruko Sugimura, Yoko Naito, Ken Mitsuda, Kinuyo Tanaka, Chishu Ryu, Yoshitaka Zushi.

### 25. Dodesukaden (*Dodesukaden*), October 27, 1970

244 minutes. Original negative in existence; prints in general circulation. A Yonki no Kai/Toho Production. Distributed by Toho. No U.S. distribution.

Produced by Yoichi Matsue. Scenario by Akira Kurosawa, Hideo Oguni, Shinobu Hashimoto. After stories by Shugoro Yamamoto. Photographed by Takao Saito (standard screen/Eastmancolor). Art Direction by Yoshiro and Shinobu Muraki. Sound Recording by Fumio Yamaguchi. Music by Toru Takemitsu.

With Yoshitaka Zushi, Kin Sugai, Junzaburo Ban, Kiyoko Tange, Michiko Hino, Tape Shimokawa, Keishi Furuyama, Hisashi Igawa, Hideko Okiyama, Kunie Tanaka, Jitsuko Yoshimura, Shinsuke Minami, Yoko Kusunoki, Toshiyuki Tonomura, Miika Oshida, Satoshi Hasegawa, Kumiko Ono, Tatsuhiko Yagishita, Tatsuo Matsumura, Tsuji Imura, Tomoko Yamazaki, Masahiko Kametani, Noboru Mitani, Hiroyuki Kawase, Hiroshi Akutagawa, Tomoko Naraoka, Atsushi Watanabe, Jerry Fujio, Sanji Kojima, Masahiko Tanimura, Kazuo Kato, Akemi Negishi, Michiko Araki, Shoichi Kuwayama, Kamatari Fujiwara.

# Selected Bibliography

BOOKS, ETC., DEVOTED TO JAPANESE CINEMA

Anderson, Joseph L., and Donald Richie. *The Japanese Film: Art and Industry*. Tokyo: Charles E. Tuttle Co., 1959 (out of print); New York: Grove Press, 1960. Provides the best background for the Japanese cinema in general.

Giuglaris, Shinobu, and Marcel. *Le cinéma japonais*. Paris: Editions du Cerf, 1956. Partial, but interesting, view.

"Le cinéma japonais." *Cinéma '55*, no. 6 (June–July 1955). Excellent source reference work.

Richie, Donald. *Japanese Movies*. Tokyo: Japan Travel Bureau, 1961 (out of print).

———. *The Japanese Movie: An Illustrated History*. Tokyo: Kodansha International, 1965.

———. *Japanese Cinema: Film Style and National Character*. New York: Doubleday, 1971. A very substantial recasting of *Japanese Movies;* offers the most complete critical evaluation.

Steinberg, Heinz. *Japanische Filmkunst*. Kiel: University of Kiel, 1959. Partial, but interesting, view.

Svenson, Arne. *Japan*. Screen Series. Cranbury, N.J.: A. S. Barnes, 1971. An indispensable reference guide.


BOOKS, ETC., DEVOTED TO KUROSAWA

*Akira Kurosawa*. Tokyo: Toho, Publications Section, n.d. (ca. 1960). The prime source for Kurosawa's opinions of his own work. This mimeographed pamphlet was printed for Toho and is not available to the general public.

"Akira Kurosawa." *Études cinématographiques* (Paris), nos. 30–31 (Spring 1964). A collection of essays on the director's work, drawn mainly from French sources; most reprints, but some original material.

"Akira Kurosawa" (in Japanese). *Kinema Jumpo* (Tokyo), no. 338 (special issue; March 25, 1963). Collection of Japanese criticism and interview with the director. Very important as primary source material.

Arbeitsgemeinschaft für Filmfragen an der Universität zu Köln. *Der Japanische Film. I: Akira Kurosawa/Dokumentation*. Cologne: University of Cologne, 1962. A somewhat sketchy bibliographical collection of opinions on Kurosawa, gathered from various sources, coupled with credits and casts of films.

Ezratty, Sacha. *Kurosawa*. Paris: Éditions Universitaires, 1964. A somewhat popular account of the director's career and works, marred by some errors and distinguished by some fresh insights.

*Kurosawa*. Uppsala, Sweden: Uppsala Studenters Filmstudio, n.d. A series of notes to accompany a showing of Kurosawa's films, this publication is important in that it gives the only available English translation of Shinbi Iida's *Kurosawa* (containing much *Rashomon* material), which originally appeared in *Cinema* 1, no. 5, and Donald Richie's *Kurosawa on Kurosawa,* which originally appeared in *Sight and Sound,* Spring–Summer, Fall–Winter, 1964, as well as the Shirai, Shibata, Yamada, "Entretien avec Akira Kurosawa," which originally appeared in *Cahiers du Cinéma,* no. 182, 1966. Contains articles in Swedish, English, and French.

Kurosawa, Akira. *The Complete Works of Akira Kurosawa*. Tokyo: Kinema Jumpo Sha, 1971–72. Invaluable as primary source material. All the scripts of Kurosawa (except for several of the early films), published in a bilingual format (Japanese and English), with a still for every scene. Eventually to consist of twelve volumes in all; six have been published as of 1972. All inquiries concerning this material should be addressed to Kinema Jumpo Sha, Shiba Park Building, Shiba, 9–3 Sakae-cho, Monato-ku, Tokyo, Japan.

Richie, Donald. *Kurosawa Retrospektive*. XI International Filmfestspiele, Berlin. Munich: Betafilm, 1961. The program book for the Kurosawa retrospective in Berlin in 1961, including bilingual (German and English) notes on all the films made to that date.

Sato, Tadao. *The World of Akira Kurosawa (Akira Kurosawa no Sekkai).* Tokyo: Sanichishobo, 1968. The finest Japanese-language evaluation of Kurosawa and his films. Contains a wealth of critical insight and much documentary material not available elsewhere.

"Two Japanese: Kurosawa and Mifune" (in Japanese). *Kinema Jumpo,* no. 10 (special issue; September 5, 1964). Collection of Japanese criticism and interview with Kurosawa.

ARTICLES AND REVIEWS ON KUROSAWA AND HIS WORK

"Akira Kurosawa." *The East* 1, no. 6 (July 1965).

Anderson, Joseph L. "When the Twain Meet: Hollywood's Remake of *Seven Samurai." Film Quarterly,* Spring 1962. An examination of the Kurosawa and Sturges films, with the conclusion that Kurosawa is a real *auteur* and Sturges a major talent hindered and helped by studio, writers, producers, etc.

Anderson, Joseph L., and Donald Richie. "Traditional Theater and the Film in Japan." [*Rashomon,* etc.]. *Film Quarterly* 12, no. 1 (Fall 1958). An examination of Japanese-theater influence on Japanese film, with the conclusion that there is little except self-consciously, that reasons for seeming influence lie in the fact that the mind making the Kabuki or Noh is the same cultural mind making the movies.

Anderson, Lindsay. "Two Inches Off the Ground" [*Ikiru*]. *Sight and Sound* 27, no. 3 (Winter 1957–58). An examination of Kurosawa's *Ikiru* in the company of Ozu and Mizoguchi: a definition of the transcendent experience. Hence the Zen description of *satori:* two inches off the ground but otherwise normal.

Bernhardt, William. *"Ikiru." Film Quarterly,* Summer 1960.

————. *"The Throne of Blood." For Film,* Winter 1962.

Billard, Pierre. *"Un mervielleux dimanche." Cinéma '64,* no. 83 (February 1964).

Delling, Manfred. "Hört dieses Eland denn niemals auf?" [*Seven Samurai*]. *Die Welt* (Hamburg), August 4, 1962.

El-Bahi, Abdelhelil. *"Rashomon." I.D.H.E.C.* (Paris), no. 145.

Gaffary, F. "Les deux disages d'Akira Kurosawa." *Positif,* no. 22 (1957).

Gregor, Ulrich. "Akira Kurosawa—Portrait." *Filmkritik* 7, no. 84 (December 1963). A short portrait of Kurosawa the man and his style, the author seeing one the result of the other.

Hull, David Stewart. *"The Bad Sleep Well."* U.C.L.A. Film Series Notes, Fall 1962.

"Kurosawa: Japan's Poet Laureate of Film." *Show Business Illustrated,* April 1962.

Leirens, Jean. "Akira Kurosawa." *Amis du Film,* no. 69 (September 1961).

Leonard, Harold. *"Ikiru."* U.C.L.A. Film Series Notes (first American showing), March 25, 1956.

Leyda, Jay. "The Films of Kurosawa." *Sight and Sound* 24 (October–December 1954). An excellent examination of the director's work (1950–54) with an emphasis upon the liberal social philosophy of *Seven Samurai.*

McVay, Douglas. "The Rebel in Kimono." *Films and Filming,* no. 10–11 (July–August 1961).

Moullet, Luc. "La rétrospective Kurosawa à la Cinémathèque." *Cahiers du cinéma,* no. 68 (February 1957).

Richardson, Tony. *"Seven Samurai."* *Sight and Sound,* Spring 1955. An appreciation of *Seven Samurai* from the filmmaker's point of view, with interesting notes on Kurosawa's use of camera in this film.

Richie, Donald. "Akira Kurosawa." *Who's Who in Japan.* Tokyo, 1960. Standard format biography and appreciation; emphasis on Kurosawa's individuality as a Japanese filmmaker.

———. "Akira Kurosawa." *Orient-West* (Tokyo), Summer 1962. Popular article on director with particular emphasis on *Ikiru* and other socially conscious films.

———. "Dostoevsky with a Japanese Camera." *Horizon* (New York), Spring 1962. Article on Kurosawa with special emphasis on his particular humanism, his love for and emulation of the Russian author, etc.

———. "Kurosawa: A Foreign View of the Japanese View" (in Japanese). *Kinema Jumpo,* no. 338 (March 25, 1963). An examination of Japanese and Western criticism on Kurosawa with the conclusion that the Americans and Europeans can appreciate more astutely since they are not biased by the "Japaneseness" of Kurosawa.

————. "Heaven and Hell" [*High and Low*]. *Films and Filming*, January 1963. An account of a trip to Toho to watch the filming of *High and Low* with many insights into Kurosawa's way of working.

Sadoul, Georges. "Existe-t-il un néo-réalism japonais?" [*Rashomon,* etc.]. *Cahiers du cinéma*, no. 28 (November 1953). The conclusion is that the neo-realism exists and is found mainly in films of a leftist persuasion, among which *Rashomon* is to be classed as a "liberal" film.

————. "*Rashomon.*" *Les lettres françaises*, no. 354. An examination of the film as indicative of postwar Japanese thought, with particular emphasis upon lack of social responsibility. Otherwise, the film is well explicated.

————. "*Les sept samouraïs.*" *Les lettres françaises*, no. 597. *Seven Samurai* as a continuation of the "tendency films" of prewar Japanese and European cinema.

Silverstein, Norman. "Kurosawa's Detective-Story Parables" [*Stray Dog, High and Low*]. *Japan Quarterly* 12, no. 3 (July–September 1965). An interesting comparison of Kurosawa's detective-story films with their sources and the European model of Simenon, concluding that Kurosawa does something very personal and special with his material.

Vance, James. "*The Lower Depths.*" *Film Quarterly*, Winter 1959.

Yvoire (d'), Jean. "*Les sept samouraïs.*" *Télérama*, no. 679.

Young, Vernon. "*The Hidden Fortress.*" *Hudson Review* 14, no. 2.

Zendel, José. "*Rashomon.*" *Les lettres françaises*, no. 411.

# Index[1]

[1] Index covers pp. 1–139 only and excludes references to Akira Kurosawa and *Rashomon*.